LIVING IN TOUCH WITH GOD

LIVING IN TOUCH WITH GOD

LARRY RICHARDS

PYRANEE
BOOKS

Zondervan Publishing House
Grand Rapids, Michigan

LIVING IN TOUCH WITH GOD
(adapted from *A Practical Theology of Spirituality* by Lawrence O. Richards
[Grand Rapids: Zondervan Publishing House, 1987].)

This is a Pyranee Book
Published by the Zondervan Publishing House,
1415 Lake Drive, S.E., Grand Rapids, Michigan 49506

Library of Congress Cataloging in Publication Data

Richards, Larry, 1931–
    Living in touch with God.

    Adaptation of: A practical theology of spirituality.
© 1987.
    1. Spirituality.   I. Richards, Larry, 1931–
Practical theology of spirituality.   II. Title.
BV4501.2.R5123 1988   248   87-34071
ISBN 0-310-39141-5

Edited by Linda Vanderzalm

Designed by Ann Cherryman

Printed in the United States of America

88 89 90 91 92 93 / CH / 10 9 8 7 6 5 4 3 2 1

CONTENTS

Introduction

This short book will take a look at Christian spirituality—what it means for us to live our human lives in touch with God. When we receive Christ, we become one with Him. But whether or not we *experience* that union, whether or not we live our human lives in union with the Lord is a matter of personal choice and discipline.

Christian spirituality is unique in that it calls on us to live a truly human life. We are not called to leave the world or to reject our humanity; the spiritual Christian is fully involved in his or her world. Christian spirituality is unique also in that we should express our union with God in our everyday lives. And our model for spirituality is Jesus. Just as Jesus lived His human life in intimate union with the Father, so we are to live our human lives in intimate touch with God. And the goal of spirituality is Christlikeness. We long to become more and more like Jesus.

But how can we live our human lives in touch—in union—with the Lord? What are the steps we can take to help us experience union with God in each aspect of our humanity? First, we must choose to place ourselves in constant touch with Him. Then, we must be willing to develop and to exercise several spiritual disciplines.

I hope that when you read this book, you'll want to discuss its concepts with others. Perhaps a small Bible study group is the ideal place to explore what it means to live in touch with God. If you use this book with a group, follow a simple process. Before you meet, read through one chapter. When you meet, use the "To Think About and Do" ideas at the end of each chapter as a springboard to your thinking and sharing. And most important, after your meeting, put into practice one or more of the spiritual disciplines suggested. Select one person in the group to be your partner and report to each other what happens as you practice the disciplines during a week. If you do not study the book with a group, commit yourself to some serious thinking and wrestling with the ideas presented. And commit yourself to exercising the spiritual disciplines examined in the book.

The material in this book is adapted from a more comprehensive book I recently completed: *A Practical Theology of Spirituality* (Grand Rapids: Zondervan Publishing House, 1986). If you want to explore the study of spirituality further, you may want to read this textbook, which examines many other aspects of living our human lives in union with God.

One final word. Spiritual development is by nature *growth,* and no growth takes place instantaneously. Don't expect that by reading a book like this, or by studying it with others, automatic changes will take place in your life. I hope you will find this book to be a companion that you can return to for encouragement. I hope you gradually will grow in each aspect of spirituality. And I hope you will return again and again to develop the disciplines that will enable you to experience fully your union with Jesus Christ, our Lord.

Larry Richards

1

SPIRITUALITY

Last September our Bible study group met to decide what
to study. We chatted about a number of possibilities. And
then someone suggested spirituality.

"What is spirituality, anyway?"

*"I know people who think they are spiritual if they pray a lot
or if they can quote lots of verses."*

"Or go to church a lot."

"How does a person become more spiritual?"

These were just some of the comments. But underlying
all of them was the shared conviction that we *need* to be
spiritual. No one was quite sure what it means to be
spiritual, though we all had impressions and ideas. But we
all knew that the Christian is called to live a spiritual life,
to be a spiritual person, to grow spiritually.

We all know intuitively that our lives can be meaningful
only if we live them in intimate touch with our God. And
the Bible's exciting message is that we *can* live in touch
with God. We can be truly spiritual men and women. But
first we need to discover what the Bible teaches about
spirituality, and we need to rid ourselves of some false
images of what it means to be spiritual.

Jesus

If we want to see a truly spiritual person, we need to
look at Jesus. In watching Jesus and listening to His
words, we can sense the true nature of Christian spirituality. We can even see something of the kind of life you and
I are called to live as His followers.

The first thing we note is that Jesus lived His spiritual
life in the real world. He was a true human being. He was
born a baby. He grew up in a typical family, with a mom
and dad and brothers and sisters. As Jesus grew up, He

worked as a carpenter. He ate, drank, spent time with friends. He met and interacted with all sorts of people. As we read the Gospels, we realize that Jesus was a busy person, pressured by events and by the importance of His mission.

And Jesus had, and needed, His times alone with the Father. Prayer was a part of Jesus' spirituality. But Jesus did not go off on some endless retreat. Jesus' spirituality was expressed in His daily interaction with all kinds of people. This spiritual man spent endless hours healing the sick, teaching the crowds, training His disciples, and fending off the barbs and plots of His enemies. And in it all, His warmth and compassion drew the lost and needy to Him.

In Jesus we see a striking kind of spirituality—a spirituality that is expressed by involvement in the world rather than by withdrawal from it. Jesus lived an active human life. But He lived that life in union with God. He lived in constant touch with the Father so that both His words and actions were expressions of God's own person and nature:

> "I tell you the truth, the Son can do nothing by himself; he can do only what he sees his Father doing, because whatever the Father does the Son also does. For the Father loves the Son and shows him all he does" (John 5:19–20a).

> "For I have come down from heaven not to do my will but to do the will of him who sent me" (John 6:38).

> "I do nothing on my own but speak just what the Father has taught me. The one who sent me is with me; he has not left me alone, for I always do what pleases him" (John 8:28b–29).

> "When a man believes in me, he does not believe in me only, but in the one who sent me. When he looks at me, he sees the one who sent me" (John 12:44–45).

"Don't you know me, Philip, even after I have been among you such a long time? Anyone who has seen me has seen the Father. How can you say, 'Show us the Father'? Don't you believe that I am in the Father, and that the Father is in me? The words I say to you are not just my own. Rather, it is the Father, living in me, who is doing his work. Believe me when I say that I am in the Father and the Father is in me" (John 14:9–11a).

These statements help us understand the unique nature of Christ's spirituality. In all Jesus did and said, He reflected His Father's will; His whole life was lived in submission to His Father's direction. He lived in total union with His Father. Spirituality is the same for you and me. It is living our human life in this world, in touch with God. It is being aware of God's presence, responding to His guidance, doing what pleases Him.

Spiritual vs. Material†

Many religious people have turned away from the kind of spirituality we see exhibited in Jesus. Early in the Christian era, distorted notions of spirituality infected the young church. Some people believed in two realities: one "spiritual" and the other "material." They thought of these two realities as opposed to each other. The spiritual realm, the dwelling place of God, was good, while the material realm was evil.

In response to this kind of thinking, the people completely separated the spiritual from the material. They thought their physical bodies were "evil," while their immaterial souls within their bodies were "good." They

[1] Word studies, Scripture explications, and theological discussions that are taken from the author's *Practical Theology of Spirituality* (Grand Rapids: Zondervan Publishing House, 1987) are noted in this book by †. This discussion on "Spiritual vs. Material" is based on chapter 4, pp. 50–53.

believed that to be truly spiritual, they had to divorce the inner self from bodily life. Thus they withdrew from life in the world, retreating to monastery cells and separating their spiritual duties from their daily lives. This ascetic self-denial, they believed, would lead to personal spiritual development.

This belief also led to a terrible heresy in the early church. If the spiritual realm (where God and good reside) is so completely separated from the material (evil) realm, then God never would become involved in the physical universe. Therefore, Jesus could not be both God and man, for that would mean God took on a physical nature—that the "good" bonded with "evil." As a result, those who rigorously separated the spiritual from the material began to deny Jesus. Perhaps He was a lesser being, an angel perhaps, but never God! Or perhaps He was simply an immaterial shadow, an image that *appeared* to be human.

The apostle Paul addresses this heresy in his letter to the Colossians. There he insists that Jesus is the exact representation [*eikon*] of the invisible God. Paul finds no conflict between the material and spiritual realms, for it is "by Christ's physical body through death" that you and I are presented to God the Father "holy in his sight, without blemish and free from accusation" (Col. 1:22).

Paul's point is important. The material world, where we live out our ordinary human lives, is *not* in conflict with the spiritual world, where God dwells. In fact, the material world is the very location God chose to accomplish His spiritual purposes! And He began to accomplish that spiritual purpose by sending Jesus, the God-Man— one person who was both full deity and true humanity. As the Bible says, "For in Christ all the fullness of the Deity lives in bodily form, and you have been given fullness in Christ" (Col. 2:9–10a).

Paul then goes on to correct the notion that Christian

spirituality calls for ascetic self-denial. He tells us not to confuse spirituality with the "dos and don'ts" imposed on them by "human commands and teachings" (Col. 2:22b). Such practices may look impressive, but they "lack any value" for the person who desires to live in vital touch with God (Col. 2:23b).

Paul has made two important points. First, he has shown us in the person of Christ that God has in fact chosen the material world as the location to accomplish His spiritual purposes. Second, Paul has shown us that ascetic self-denial or withdrawal is not how Christians live in touch with God.

Then Paul goes on to give a brief sketch of how we *can live* in touch with God. And what Paul focuses on is just what we have seen in Jesus. Right here—in this world, in our relationships to other people—we are to live a life that expresses the nature and character of God!

> Therefore, as God's chosen people, holy and dearly loved, clothe yourselves with compassion, kindness, humility, gentleness and patience. Bear with each other and forgive whatever grievances you may have against one another. Forgive as the Lord forgave you. And over all these virtues put on love, which binds them all together in perfect unity.

> Let the peace of Christ rule in your hearts, since as members of one body you were called to peace. And be thankful. Let the word of Christ dwell in you richly as you teach and admonish one another with all wisdom, and as you sing psalms, hymns and spiritual songs with gratitude in your hearts to God. And whatever you do, whether in word or deed, do it all in the name of the Lord Jesus, giving thanks to God the Father through him (Col. 3:12–17).

An Incarnational Spirituality

What Paul says in Colossians helps us understand Christian spirituality. True spirituality does not separate the spiritual from the material. We believe that God created our world and that in Jesus, He entered our world as a true human being. We believe that God's spiritual purposes were and are achieved in the universe in which you and I now live. In fact, Jesus' incarnation shows us just how important life in this world can be! What we say and do in our lives on earth is the very heart of spirituality.

In Jesus we see that God's will for His people is not retreat or isolation. Ascetic *disconnection* from the real world is not Christian. Instead, Christianity calls for *connection*—connection to God and connection to the world in which we live. Jesus was vitally connected to the people and issues of His time. He was totally involved in His world. And He was totally connected to God. We too must discover that living in intimate touch with God means becoming totally involved with others as we speak and act "in the name of the Lord Jesus" (Col. 3:17).

In its most basic sense, Christian spirituality is incarnational. In Jesus, God broke into our world of space and time to live a truly spiritual life in a sin-warped society. We too are called to an incarnational spirituality, to live out God's will in a world that remains warped and twisted by sin.

OUR UNION WITH JESUS†

Jesus' life on earth was a truly human life, lived in union with God the Father. That's the significance of those verses we looked at earlier. Jesus did nothing by Himself; He did only what He saw the Father doing (John 5:19). Jesus said He came to do His Father's will (John 6:38). The Father was always with Jesus, for Jesus always did what pleased the Father (John 8:29). The union of the two was so perfect that anyone looking at Jesus could see God

†This discussion is based on chapter 4, pp. 53–56.

(John 12:45). And all this was because Jesus is "in" the Father and the Father is "in" Jesus. All Jesus did as a human being expressed God, who was living in Jesus, doing His work (John 14:10).

At first this seems to be an impossible task for you and me. If Christian spirituality calls for this kind of bonding with God—something that was natural for Jesus—how can we ever live a spiritual life? The amazing answer comes in a prayer Jesus offered for all who trust in Him. In this prayer Jesus sums up the nature of Christian spirituality, and He helps us understand the basis on which we can live a truly spiritual life.

As you read Jesus' prayer, note the following important points: Jesus calls us to live *in* this world but not *of* it. Jesus desires us to be sanctified, to be set apart fully to God. Jesus asks that we may be "one" with Him *in the same way that He has been one with the Father in His life on earth!* It is as we are brought to complete unity (with Jesus) that we will express God in this world just as Jesus did. Through us the world will know that the Father truly sent Jesus.

> "They are not of the world any more than I am of the world. My prayer is not that you take them out of the world but that you protect them from the evil one. They are not of the world, even as I am not of it. Sanctify them by the truth; your word is truth. As you sent me into the world, I have sent them into the world. For them I sanctify myself, that they too may be truly sanctified" (John 17:14b–19).

> "I pray . . . that all of them may be one, Father, just as you are in me and I am in you. May they also be in us so that the world may believe that you have sent me. I have given them the glory that you gave me, that they may be one as we are one: I in them and you in me. May they be brought to complete unity to let the world know that you sent me and have loved them even as you have loved me" (John 17:20b–23).

Many Christians believe this passage refers to the unity between members of the body of Christ on earth. Perhaps this is implied, but the clear focus of the prayer is on our union with God. As Jesus was in the Father and the Father in Jesus, so the New Testament teaches that you and I are in Him.

The glory of God's gift to us is the glory of a real and present union with God. The wonder of our relationship with Jesus is that *we can be one with Jesus:* "I in them and you in me."

"OK," one of our group objected. "I buy this idea of our union with God. After all, the Bible talks a lot about being 'in Christ.' But if we've got that kind of relationship with Jesus, why isn't spirituality easier for us? How come it's something we have to work at?"

The reason, of course, isn't all that hard to understand. Our union with Jesus, that real union that does exist, is the foundation for all our spiritual experience. Only because we truly are united to Him do the spiritual and material universe actually touch within us. But we must go on to build on that foundation. We must learn to let the spiritual reality dominate, to let the will of God find free expression in our lives, just as Jesus let the will of God find full expression in His every word and act.

John 17 isn't, of course, the only New Testament passage about our union with Jesus. Romans 6 exultantly shouts that we can be freed from the domination of the "old self" in us, scarred as it is with sinful thoughts and deeds, to live a truly righteous life. But even here Paul stresses the importance of choice. We are to choose not to yield to our sinful urges. We are to choose to yield to God, surrendering every part of our bodies to Him as instruments of righteousness (Rom. 6:1–14).

The same theme is emphasized in Philippians 2. "If you have any encouragement from being united with Christ," Paul begins, "if any comfort from his love . . . make my joy complete by *being* like-minded, *having* the same love, *being* one in spirit and purpose" (Phil. 2:1–2, italics added). We who are united to Christ are to "do nothing out of selfish ambition or vain conceit, but in humility consider others better than [ourselves]" (Phil. 2:3). As we adopt the attitude of Jesus, humbling ourselves to live an obedient life as Jesus did, we will "work out [express] [our] salvation with fear and trembling" confident that "it is God who works in [us] to will and to act according to his good purpose" (Phil. 2:12b–13).

Yes, you and I are bonded to Jesus. We have a real and present union with our Lord. Because of Jesus, the spiritual and material realms touch within us.

But our challenge is to live a life that is surrendered to and guided by the spiritual reality. Like Jesus, we are to experience our union with God, and aware of His presence, we are to do His will. We are to live our human life in union with God.

The Spiritual Life

At this point we can draw together a few insights into Christian spirituality. First, true spirituality is modeled by Jesus Christ, who lived a truly human life in perfect union with God the Father. Every notion about spirituality must be tested against Jesus and the kind of life He lived in total harmony with the Father's will.

Second, our spirituality is essentially the same kind that we see modeled by Jesus. *Our spirituality is expressed in our human lives,* not by withdrawing from what it means to be a human being in the real world. This spirituality is rooted in a union with Jesus that is like His union with the Father. Because our union with Jesus is real, we can respond to His will, speak His words, and do the things that please Him. Our response to God is the key to *experiencing* the union that does exist.

Third, we must take very seriously the idea that living a

human life is central to Christian spirituality. The Bible calls us to imitate our God and to "live a life of love, just as Christ loved us" (Eph. 5:2a). We are to put off the old self, corrupted by its deceitful desires, and "be made new in the attitude of [our] minds; and to put on the new self, created to be like God in true righteousness and holiness" (Eph. 4:23–24). We are to remember that Jesus was "leaving [us] an example, that [we] should follow in his steps" (1 Peter 2:21b), so that we will learn "to live . . . [our] earthly life [not] for evil human desires, but rather for the will of God" (1 Peter 4:2). Yes, Christian spirituality *is* living an earthly life, but living it by God's will.

"So we're right back to the beginning, aren't we?" Steve observed. *"We know what spirituality is. It's living our everyday life in union with Jesus. But what does it mean?"*

And then everyone responded.

"Does it mean praying more?"

"Maybe. But it's got to mean more than that. For one thing, Jesus spent a lot of time with people. And those Bible verses we looked at say a lot about things like kindness and forgiveness."

"Since Jesus was a human being, I mean really human, maybe before we can understand spirituality, we've got to know more about what it means to be a human being. What's so special about that human life we're supposed to live in union with God?"

"Let's follow up on that a minute. In the beginning, God made human beings special. He made us in His image, with personal responsibility and a capacity for fellowship with Him. Then sin came in. To be human means we have to deal with our sin—and with the sin of others around us. So maybe what we need to do to understand how to live in touch with God is to focus on special challenges we face as human beings. Then we can see how to respond to those challenges in God's way!"

And that is just what we did. And that is what this book is about. It's about what is so special about living a truly human life in the real world and about how to live that human life in union with, in constant touch with God.

How wonderful to know that through Jesus we truly are bonded to our God and that the foundation for a vital spiritual life exists. We have been united with Jesus by faith. And now, by faith's response of obedience to God's Word, we can go on to experience that union and to live the truly spiritual life for which we yearn.

TO THINK ABOUT AND DO

1. Who is the most "spiritual" person you've known? Jot down words that describe him or her. Tell other people about this person and listen to their descriptions of "spiritual" people they have known. Then discuss: What ideas of "spirituality" are assumed in your descriptions?

2. Read Colossians 3:12–17. Work with a friend to build a personality sketch of a "spiritual Christian" from these two short paragraphs.

3. When the Pharisees criticized Jesus for eating with tax collectors and "sinners" (see Luke 27–32), they did so because they had a particular view of spirituality. How would you describe this view? What do you think was wrong with it?

4. In what area of your life do you need to be more spiritual?

2

INTIMACY

"I remember times in my life when I felt very close to God. It was as if He was right there in the room with me. His presence was so real that I found myself wanting to talk out loud to Him."

"I've had times like that too, but not very many. That's the kind of closeness I would like to experience more often."

"Me too. Why don't we feel more close to God? Why do I so often feel that when I pray to Him, my prayers don't even reach the ceiling?"

Our group had touched on an important issue. If believers are bonded to God through Jesus' death, why do we often feel so distant from Him? How can we experience our union with Him in close, intimate ways?

Intimacy in Eden

To understand spiritual intimacy, we need to go back to Creation. There we see humankind created "in the image of God (Gen. 1:27b)." This significant phrase has a sharp and clear meaning. It means that God made us to be like Himself. To truly understand human nature, we can compare ourselves only to God. We human beings are more like God than we are like anything else in all of Creation.

That likeness is essentially personal. That is, like God, we are true persons, with emotions, with intelligence, with will. We are made like God, with the capacity to appreciate beauty, to take pleasure in accomplishing meaningful work, to exercise creativity, to enjoy social relationships with others of our own kind.

Looking back into those first, pregnant chapters of Genesis, we see something else. We see that because we are created in God's image, we have both the capacity and the need for personal relationship with Him. We have a deep inner need to be close to God.

In Eden, that need to be close to God was met. The Bible tells us that God spoke to Adam and Eve and that He strolled in the Garden with them "in the cool of the day (Gen. 3:8)." He didn't come to instruct them. He didn't come to question them. He didn't come to hear their requests. He came simply so that He could be *with them* and they could be *with Him*.

God came to the Garden in the cool of the day so that both He and our first parents could enjoy one another's company. He came for intimacy.

But sin shattered that original harmony. Suddenly the warmth and closeness Adam and Eve felt with God was replaced by fear. When God came to the Garden after Adam and Eve had sinned, they both fled, terrified of the One whose love they had experienced. But God would not be put off. God sought them out, and making history's first sacrifice, He covered the sinning pair with animal skins. Thousands of years later, God fulfilled the commitment this original act implied. In the person of Jesus, God came to seek and to save those who were lost. In His death, Jesus provided the ultimate covering for our sins. And by His death, Jesus restored us to that original, close relationship to Him.

Jesus came and died to restore our capacity for fellowship with God. Jesus came to restore our intimacy with Him. Jesus came so that we once again can walk with God in the cool of our day.

Human beings were created to experience fellowship with God. To live a truly human life is to live in intimate, personal relationship with our Creator—a Creator who has in Jesus become our Redeemer.

Expressing Intimacy†

The truth is that God is with us every day, in every circumstance. He is there—whether or not we recognize His presence. God has done His part; it is our responsibility to learn to be aware of His closeness to us.

When we want to get close to another human being, we spend time with that person. We talk to each other, learning about each other's lives and hopes and struggles. The more we talk and listen, the more we learn about each other. And the more we share from the heart, the closer we feel to each other.

The same is true of our relationship to God. The more we recognize His presence with us, the more we will want to be with Him, talking to Him and listening to His voice. But many of us don't know how to talk to God—to pray this way. We want to be close to Him, but we don't know how to pray what some spiritual writers call "prayers of the heart." We don't know how to be intimate with God.

The Bible uses many different Hebrew and Greek words to discuss prayer. Together these words show us how rich and complex our relationship to God may be. In the Old Testament, *pālal* and its derivatives express a call to God, a request for Him to see a present need and act on it. This word suggests not only a deep awareness of dependence on the Lord but also the petitioner's humble spirit. *Na'* is a simple expression of entreaty, while *'aṯar* implies intensity and earnestness. *Šā'al* means "ask" or "inquire" and often is linked with seeking guidance. Still another word, *'ānâh,* indicates an urgent call to God. *Pāga'* is used of intercession, while *hānan* is an appeal to God's grace and mercy.

We see a similar variety of meanings in the New Testament. The word that indicates prayer in general is *proseuchomai,* which suggests the warmth of genuine

†This discussion is based on chapter 8, pp. 99–104.

conversation. *Aiteō* means to "ask" or "request"; *deomai* is the request of a person deeply aware of need. *Erōtaō* means "ask" or "request," and when it is used with *entynchanō,* it means "intercede."

So it's clear that our prayer relationship with God truly is varied and complex. But none of these words conveys the wonder of the intimacy we sense in some of the psalms and the intimacy we see so clearly in the life of Jesus.

Listen to the psalmists' hearts and sense the intimacy of their relationship to God. These are words of people who have rediscovered Eden in their hearts and have found in prayer a way to walk again with God.

> How great is your goodness,
>   which you have stored up for those who fear you,
> which you bestow in the sight of men
>   on those who take refuge in you.
> In the shelter of your presence you hide them
>   from the intrigues of men;
> in your dwelling you keep them safe
>   from accusing tongues (Ps. 31:19–20).

> I will remember the deeds of the LORD;
>   yes, I will remember your miracles of long ago.
> I will meditate on all your works
>   and consider all your mighty deeds (Ps. 77:11–12).

> O God, you are my God,
>   earnestly I seek you;
> my soul thirsts for you,
>   my body longs for you,
> in a dry and weary land
>   where there is no water.
> I have seen you in the sanctuary
>   and beheld your power and your glory.
> Because your love is better than life,
>   my lips will glorify you.
> I will praise you as long as I live,

and in your name I will lift up my hands.
My soul will be satisfied
    as with the richest of foods;
  with singing lips my mouth will praise you.
On my bed I remember you;
  I think of you through the watches of the night.
Because you are my help,
  I sing in the shadow of your wings.
My soul clings to you;
  Your right hand upholds me (Ps. 63:1–8).

Yet I am always with you;
  you hold me by my right hand.
You guide me with your counsel,
  and afterward you will take me into glory.
Whom have I in heaven but you?
  And earth has nothing I desire besides you.
My flesh and my heart may fail,
  but God is the strength of my heart
  and my portion forever.
But as for me, it is good to be near God.
  I have made the Sovereign LORD my refuge;
  I will tell of all your deeds (Ps. 73:23–26, 28).

Jesus and Intimacy†

Jesus is our model of the human life lived in union with God. What do we learn about prayer of the heart, about intimacy, by looking at His life here on earth?

Most of Jesus' prayers recorded in the Gospels are public prayers. But we know that Jesus often found time for private, personal, intimate times with His Father. For instance, after one especially busy day, Jesus "went up on a mountainside by himself to pray" (Matt. 14:23b). On another occasion, "very early in the morning, while it was still dark, Jesus got up, left the house and went off to a solitary place, where he prayed" (Mark 1:35). Luke says

†This discussion is based on chapter 8, pp. 104–106.

that as more and more crowds were drawn to Him, "Jesus often withdrew to lonely places and prayed" (Luke 5:16). Luke also tells us that, as Jesus' enemies were plotting how to kill Him, our Lord "went out to a mountainside to pray, and spent the night praying to God" (Luke 6:12).

Luke, whose writings stress Jesus' humanity, also tells us that Jesus traveled to the Mount of Transfiguration "to pray" and "as he was praying, the appearance of his face changed, and his clothes became as bright as a flash of lightning" (Luke 9:29). Luke is also the one who adds that when Jesus had been "praying in a certain place," His disciples finally asked the Lord to teach them to pray, "just as John taught his disciples" (Luke 11:1).

In each of these references, the gospel writers use *proseuchomai,* which, although it is the New Testament's most general word for prayer, suggests warm and intimate conversation. It is striking that each writer uses the same term (*proseuchomai*) in describing the scene in Gethsemane (Matt. 26; Mark 14; Luke 22). But *proseuchomai* is *not* found in Jesus' prayer recorded in John 17. There Jesus is said to have looked up and "said." And in the body of the prayer, Jesus uses the word *erōtaō,* which means "request" or "intercede for."

What conclusions can we draw from the Gospel portraits of Jesus at prayer? First of all, we see that even though Jesus lived in perfect union with the Father, Christ still needed time for intimacy with God. He needed time for prayer of the heart. This need was especially great when Jesus felt intense pressure. If Jesus needed time simply to be with God, how much more do you and I need to take time to be with Him!

Second, we have no direct record of what Jesus said and did in His intimate times with the Lord. But we do have vital clues. Those clues are found first in noting that Jesus' times of personal, intimate prayer are identified by *proseuchomai* (intimate, warm conversation) and then noting that two of His recorded prayers are marked by this same identification! The first prayer so identified is what we know as "the Lord's Prayer" (Matt. 6). This is the familiar prayer that Jesus taught His disciples. Because this teaching came just after He returned from a time of intimacy with the Father, it seems reasonable that Jesus taught his disciples *how to pray as He had been praying.* The second prayer is Jesus' prayer in Gethsemane (Matt. 26). It is clearly a prayer of the heart; a moment of deep pain has stimulated a most intimate cry.

When we compare the two prayers, we begin to sense elements involved in prayer of the heart.

Lord's Prayer Matt. 6	Gethsemane Matt. 26	Prayer of the Heart
"Our Father in Heaven,"	"My Father . . ."	Come, resting in personal relationship.
"Hallowed be your name,"	[Implied in Jesus' submission]	Come, acknowledging God, honoring Him as God.
"Your kingdom come, your will be done on earth as it is in heaven."	"Not as I will, but as you will."	Come, submitting to Him, surrendering yourself and your will.
"Give us today our daily bread."		Come, acknowledging dependence on God, expressing trust in Him.
"Forgive us our debts, as we also have forgiven our debtors."		Come, accepting God's forgiveness and freely extending it to others.
"And lead us not into temptation, but deliver us from the evil one."	[Jesus urges the three to pray so they "will not fall into temptation."]	Come, submitting to God's leading, relying always on His protection.

What we see is that the practice of intimate prayer simply calls on us to approach God, acknowledging who He is and what our relationship to Him is. In intimate prayer we submit our wills to God, allowing Him to work His will through us. We surrender our bodily nature, trusting that He will meet our daily needs. We surrender our pride, acknowledging that we are creatures who constantly need forgiveness and that we live with others who are as needy as we are. And we surrender our future to God, committing ourselves to follow His leading.

In these moments of surrender and release, we find our hearts warmed—warmed and tuned to praise the One whose love enables us to experience Him in a deeper, fresher way.

Rediscovering Eden

In Jesus' life we find some steps to help us slip back into the intimacy of Eden. God is willing, even eager to walk with us. We need to remember that prayer of the heart is not an "asking" kind of prayer: it is prayer simply for the sake of "being with" our God. And to begin, we need only to practice some disciplines that can enrich this beautiful, simple, yet vital type of prayer.

Make intimacy a priority. No one should look at this kind of prayer as a casual, "when I've time" kind of prayer. Unless you and I specifically set aside time for important things, they always are crowded out by the dozens of little duties and amusements that clamor for our attention. When first practicing prayer of the heart, spend ten minutes just to be with God. As the discipline grows, increase the time to thirty or forty-five minutes. Where and when you meet with God is important. Choose a time of the day when you are least likely to be distracted or interrupted. Then find a quiet place, a soothing place away from interruptions.

There and then, we simply open our awareness to Him. Not to ask. Not even to share. Just to be with Him.

Develop a pattern.† Most people find that some kind of pattern in prayer is best while growing in our capacity for intimacy. Again, most people encourage an initial quieting or self-emptying. Deep breathing is often suggested as an aid. For instance, we can combine breathing with a meditation, such as this one on the Lord's prayer.

Breathe in deeply	Breathe out deeply
Father, your will be done	I surrender my will to you.
Father, give this day's bread.	I surrender my fears to you.
Father, forgive my sins.	I surrender my pride to you.
Father, lead me not into temptation.	I surrender my future to you.

Repeat this meditation, breathing deeply and slowly, consciously surrendering yourself to God, releasing tensions and fears and even your will so that you will be able to concentrate on Him alone.

Learn to meditate. Meditation is focusing your attention on God, and especially on His special qualities or traits. The Psalms are a great aid to meditation; so is memorization of Scripture. As you focus on a word or concept, a trait or quality of the Lord, simply let your mind and heart be filled with its revelation of the God you are now "with."

For instance, memorize Psalm 31:19–20. Each day repeat its verses, but let your attention be fixed on just one of the italicized words or phrases each day.

†The following exercises are taken from chapter 8, pp. 106–108.

How great is your *goodness,*
  which you have stored up for those who *fear* you,
which you bestow in the sight of men
  on those who take *refuge* in you.
In the *shelter* of *your presence* you hide them
  from the intrigues of men;
in your dwelling you keep them *safe*
  from accusing tongues.

Scripture itself is probably our greatest guide and aid to prayer of the heart. We can find psalms that lift us until we can sense the presence of God. We can find images that help us realize who God is and what He means to us: shepherd, gardener, father, husband, mother hen, fortress, eagle's wings, vine, bread, altar, sacrifice. As we discover Him in His Word and in its images, our awareness of Him is nourished.

How wonderful it is to go to God's Word not only to learn but also to meet our beloved. How wonderful to let Scripture's words and images draw us into His loving presence. How wonderful to realize that God's Word is not simply a source of doctrine but also a love letter.

Express your love. Part of becoming intimate with someone is expressing your love for that person. Scripture also gives us words to express our love for God. We can "pray back" to God the words of psalms: "I love you, O LORD, my strength. [You are] my rock, my fortress and my deliverer" (Ps. 18:1–2a). "I love [you] LORD, for [you] heard my voice; [you] heard my cry for mercy. Because [you] turned [your] ear to me, I will call upon [you] as long as I live" (Ps. 116:1–2). We can find verses that will help us express our dependence on God, our trust in Him, our surrender to His will. We can memorize these verses so that we can say them aloud to God as we ride alone in the car or as we take a walk. Saying these verses to God will help us be aware of His presence with us.

Contemporary Scripture songs also are a rich guide to expressing our intimacy with God. Rather than sing *about*

God, we learn to sing *to* God, telling Him of our love and adoration for who He is. Using words from Revelation 4:11, we sing to God:

> Thou art worthy, thou art worthy,
> Thou art worthy, O Lord.
> Thou art worthy, to receive glory,
> Glory and honor and power.
> For thou hast created, hast all things created,
> For thou hast created all things.
> And for thy pleasure they are created;
> Thou art worthy, O Lord.

Or, from Philippians 2:10–11, we tell the Lord:

> You are Lord! You are Lord!
> You have risen from the dead
> And you are Lord.
> Every knee shall bow, every tongue confess
> That Jesus Christ is Lord!

Practice His presence. Learning the how of prayer of the heart takes discipline. And at first, the discipline will seem strange and somewhat forced. But in time, the daily discipline will grow into a meaningful time as we begin to recognize God's presence with us. The more we practice spending time with God, the more we will become aware of His presence with us in the everyday activities in our lives, as we drive to work, wait in line, mow the grass, relax in the evening, lie in bed. We discover that we can "be with" God in every moment of our day. We discover that the practice of His presence isn't something possible only for the unusual saint. It's possible for you, and it's possible for me.

This kind of intimacy with God is something that you and I were created for, and redeemed for. We were born, and born again, to live our human life in intimate touch with our God.

TO THINK ABOUT AND DO

1. Imagine yourself in Eden before the Fall. What would it have been like to walk with God in the cool of the day? What three words describe your feelings about that time?

2. Set aside time to be alone with God, not for traditional "devotions" or Bible reading, but simply to "be with" God, to be intimate with Him.

3. Begin to read through the Psalms, copying into a notebook verses that you can use in your time with God. Select verses that help you tell God how great, mighty, kind, merciful, forgiving, or patient He is. As you copy the verses, personalize them. If the verse says, "The Lord is kind . . . ," write, "O Lord, you are kind . . . ." This way you can "pray back" these verses to God in your time with Him.

4. Read carefully through several psalms and write down images and or symbols that the psalmists use. Then consider each image and symbol you've recorded. What does each suggest to you about God? Which adds most to your vision of who He is? Which stimulates a sense of praise?

3

REALITY

"Whenever I think about who God is—I mean who He really is—I am so overwhelmed by His greatness that I sometimes cry."

"I've had a similar experience. I find I don't have any words. I can't begin to express to Him what I think or feel."

"I have a different reaction. Whenever I think about who God really is, I am so overwhelmed by who I really am. I am so aware of my smallness, my inadequacies, my failures."

Our group had realized an important dynamic. The more we comprehend God's greatness, the more we realize our smallness. The more we grasp God's purity, the more we are aware of our own sin. The more we are in touch with the reality of who God is, the more we need to face the reality of who we are—sinners.

The Reality of Our Sin†

It is helpful for us to look at what the Bible teaches us about our sin. The Old Testament uses three basic terms to discuss sin. Each of the basic terms implies the existence of a divine standard: What is right and good is an absolute, not simply because it is revealed in the Law but because this standard is rooted in the very nature of God. It is against this standard, God Himself, that the believer learns to measure and to understand sin. One of the key Old Testament terms is *hātā'*. Used some 580 times, *hātā'* suggests falling short of the standard set in God. A second word, *pešaʿ*, suggests a rebellion, a willful revolt against the standard. Finally, *ʿāwōn* means a twisting of the standard, a moral misshapenness.

In Psalm 51, which is perhaps the Old Testament's

†This discussion is based on chapter 10, p. 124.

most significant passage about human sinfulness, each of these terms is used. That psalm reports David's confession of transgressions (*peša'*: rebelliousness), sin (*ḥāṭā'*: shortcomings), and iniquity (*'āwōn*: moral misshapenness). David realized that from the time his mother conceived him, he had been morally misshapen. He faces the fact that he both has fallen short of the divine standard and has willfully rebelled against it. Each of these is sin; each requires divine intervention for deliverance. So David turns from himself, and in this great psalm appeals to God for forgiveness and cleansing.

Have mercy on me, O God,
according to your unfailing love;
according to your great compassion
blot out my transgressions.
Wash away all my iniquity
and cleanse me from my sin.

For I know my transgressions,
and my sin is always before me.
Against you, you only, have I sinned
and done what is evil in your sight,
so that you are proved right when you speak
and justified when you judge.
Surely I was sinful at birth,
sinful from the time my mother conceived me.
Surely you desire truth in the inner parts;
you teach me wisdom in the inmost place.

Cleanse me with hyssop, and I will be clean;
wash me, and I will be whiter than snow.
Let me hear joy and gladness;
let the bones you have crushed rejoice.
Hide your face from my sins
and blot out all my iniquity (Ps. 51:1–9).

The New Testament describes human sinfulness with two major Greek word groups. One of the two is rooted in *adikia,* which means "wrongdoing," "unrighteousness," or "injustice." Words in this group view sin as willful human actions that cause harm to other persons and that violate the divine standard. The other word group is rooted in *hamartia,* which is almost always translated "sin." Words in this group incorporate the full range of meanings in each of the three basic Hebrew terms. "Sin" in the New Testament refers to our native moral misshapenness, our shortcomings, and our conscious, willful acts of rebellion against what we know is right.

While the Old Testament shows us in picture-story after picture-story (such as the story of Cain and Abel) the impact of sin in human experience, the New Testament sums up its impact on us in clear, succinct words:

> As for you, you were dead in your transgressions and sins, in which you used to live when you followed the ways of this world and of the ruler of the kingdom of the air, the spirit who is now at work in those who are disobedient. All of us also lived among them at one time, gratifying the cravings of our sinful nature and following its desires and thoughts. Like the rest, we were by nature objects of wrath (Eph. 2:1–3).

Sin does not make humans worthless. Sin does not blot out, though it distorts, the image-likeness of God. But sin's reality means that we who wish to live in touch with God must learn to deal with sin—in ourselves and in others.

Dealing with Sin†

Let's see what we can learn from Peter as he realizes the depth of his sinfulness. Peter and his partners had been fishing all night, but they had caught nothing. Early in the

---

†This discussion is based on chapter 10, pp. 127, 129–131.

morning, they returned to shore to wash out their nets. Then Jesus came, followed by crowds who pressed so close that He asked Peter to push out his boat a little from the shore. Sitting in Peter's boat, Jesus began to teach the crowds.

After He finished teaching, Jesus told Peter, "Put out into deep water, and let down the nets for a catch" (Luke 5:4b). Peter hesitated. "Master, we've worked hard all night and haven't caught anything. But because you say so, I will let down the nets" (Luke 5:5).

Still reluctant, Peter and his partners let down their nets—which became so full of fish, the two boats almost sank under their weight! When Peter came to shore, he fell on his knees and said, "Go away from me, Lord; I am a sinful man!" (Luke 5:8b).

What a strange reaction. Peter didn't get excited. He didn't tell Jesus how grateful he was for the fish. Instead, he told Jesus to go away. Intensely aware of his own sinfulness, Peter couldn't bear to be in the presence of the sinless Christ.

Peter's response to his sin is similar to Adam's reaction. Adam, too, couldn't face God after he and Eve had sinned; Adam wanted to run and hide.

Ever since Adam's first transgression, human beings have been running away from God because of a sense of sin. When we are confronted by our sinfulness, we, like Adam, try to fashion clothing from leaves to hide from ourselves and from each other.

Romans 2:15 describes the two basic ways we attempt to cover sin: "Their consciences also bearing witness, and their thoughts now *accusing,* now even *defending* them (emphasis mine)." In the larger passage, Paul explains that no person is righteous—neither the pagan nor the Jew, who knew what was right because of the Law. Paul argues that even though some people don't know the Law, they do have an inner awareness of right and wrong—the conscience. So, even though some people aren't aware that they sin—violate God's standard—their conscience tells them that they have violated their own standards.

And that is Paul's point. *Every person makes choices that violate his or her standards!* And when a person makes such a choice, his or her conscience bears witness. And when the conscience bears witness, people still try to run and hide, still try to fashion moral clothing to disguise reality from themselves and from others. Paul says that we respond to our sin in two ways: "accusing" and "defending" or self-accusation and blaming others.

Self-accusation. "Go away from me, Lord," Peter begged, "because I am a sinful man." This self-accusing person is gripped by a sense of shame, burdened with unbearable guilt. He or she is likely to feel worthless, depressed, isolated, and separated from others. People who try to deal with their sin in this way tend to become anxious and unhappy, struggling hopelessly to overcome in themselves the things that they find so unworthy. They develop an attitude of hopelessness, relying on themselves rather than on God. The self-condemning person, burdened with a poor self-image, hopelessly tries to make himself or herself worthy to stand before God.

Blaming others. When we don't want to face our own sin, we blame others. We may try to excuse ourselves by blaming others for the situations in which we made wrong choices. We may deny that an act or an attitude is sin. Our anger was "righteous." We were justified in striking out, because the other person was only getting what he or she deserved. Our action was the other person's fault, because he or she was violating our rights. We describe motives and impute all sorts of emotions and wickedness to the other person. In view of what the other person did or in view of what kind of person he or she is, our own actions were justified. But this route only traps us in a web of unreality.

How tragic. When we try to excuse sin in ourselves, no matter what the situation in which it was expressed, we are "walking in darkness," as the apostle John calls it (1 John 1:6). We have rejected reality in favor of self-deceit.

Both accusing and defending are attempts to run from our sense of sin, attempts to keep from facing not only our sinfulness but our God. Typically we respond in both ways, shifting from one to the other. But if we truly wish to walk with God, we must reject the terrible inner pressure we feel when conscience accuses us.

It is spiritual disaster to deal with our sin by accusing or by defending. Instead of attempting to disguise or deny our sin, we must face it squarely. We must acknowledge our sin—and take it immediately to God.

The Spiritual Power of Confession†

The apostle John clearly addresses the issue of what to do about our sin:

> This is the message we have heard from him and declare to you: God is light; in him there is no darkness at all. If we claim to have fellowship with him and yet walk in the darkness, we lie and do not live by the truth. But if we walk in the light, as he is in the light, we have fellowship with one another, and the blood of Jesus, his Son, purifies us from all [every] sin.
>
> If we claim to be without sin, we deceive ourselves and the truth is not in us. If we confess our sins, he is faithful and just and will forgive us our sins and purify us from all unrighteousness. If we claim we have not sinned, we make him out to be a liar and his word has no place in our lives.

†This discussion is based on chapter 10, pp. 128–130.

My dear children, I write this to you so that you will not
sin. But if anybody does sin, we have one who speaks to
the Father in our defense—Jesus Christ, the Righteous
One. He is the atoning sacrifice for our sins, and not only
for ours but also for the sins of the whole world (1 John
1:5–2:2).

John says that God is light—He sees things as they are;
He sees reality. To walk in the light means to be
completely honest with God and with ourselves. To walk
in the light is to deal with things as they really are,
without any deceit.

John's major point is that denying sin is self-deceit. It is
walking in darkness, not in light. It is only by being
honest about our sins and by confessing [*homologeō:*
literally, "acknowledging"] sins to God that He will
forgive us and cleanse us.

This vital passage clearly defines the way that we are to
deal with our sins. We are not to let them burden us with
guilt and catapult us into the morass of self-accusation.
We are not to deny our fault and plunge headlong down
the pathway of blaming others. Each of these leads us
away from God and puts us out of touch with the Lord.

Instead, we are simply to agree with God and our
conscience. We are to acknowledge, to ourselves and to
God, that a particular act or attitude is sin. And in that
simple act of confession, we are to open our hearts to
welcome God's forgiveness.

How powerful that forgiveness is! When we accept
forgiveness, we are released from guilt. When we accept
forgiveness, we need not blame ourselves, or others. And
claiming the forgiveness God has promised us, opens up
our hearts to the working of God's Spirit so that He is able
to continue purifying us within. As God does this
purifying work, we will actually become the righteous
person we so long to be.

The psalmist speaks eloquently of the joy and release

that we can feel when we face the reality of our sin, confess it to God, and experience His forgiveness:

> Blessed is he
>> whose transgressions are forgiven,
>> whose sins are covered.
> Blessed is the man
>> whose sin the LORD does not count against him
>> and in whose spirit is no deceit.
>
> When I kept silent,
>> my bones wasted away
>> through my groaning all day long.
> For day and night
>> your hand was heavy upon me;
> my strength was sapped
>> as in the heat of summer.
> Then I acknowledged my sin to you
>> and did not cover up my iniquity.
> I said, "I will confess
>> my transgressions to the LORD"—
> and you forgave
>> the guilt of my sin (Ps. 32:1–5).

This is the blessedness that we so desperately need when we sin. How wonderful to realize that we do not have to keep on carrying the weight of our failures. We can take them all to Jesus, and in His loving touch we can know the freedom that forgiveness brings.

Be sure to note the other result of walking in the light. Not only will it lead to confession and forgiveness, but it also will lead to the very intimacy with Christ we so deeply desire. "If we walk in the light, as he is in the light, we have fellowship with one another" (1 John 1:7a). If we are willing to face reality—the reality of our sin—as He does, then we can have with God the intimate relationship that is now available to us in Christ (1 John 1:1–4).

Learning How to Confess

What can we do to become sensitive to our sins and to deal with them in God's way?

Meditate on God's forgiveness. Many passages in the Bible speak of God's forgiveness. Use a concordance to locate such verses. You may want to begin by meditating on these: Ps. 32:1–5; 85:2; 86:5; 103:3, 12–14; Jer. 31:34; Mic. 7:18–19; Acts 10:43; 1 John 1:9; etc. Also read and meditate on Psalm 51 and 1 John 1:1–2:1. Saturate your mind and heart with the awareness that God doesn't condemn you for being a sinner but continues to love you completely. What God does with our sins is forgive them. We can confess our sins to God and know that He will forgive us and will take away the burden of our guilt forever.

Practice self-examination. Rather than try to hide sins and failings from yourself, spend some time each day searching for them. David prays,

Search me, O God, and know my heart;
   test me and know my anxious thoughts.
See if there is any offensive way in me,
   and lead me in the way everlasting (Ps. 139:23–24).

We can ask God's Spirit to show us sin in our lives— sins both of simply falling short and of wickedness. We can ask the Spirit to reveal warped motives we have been unaware of, self-deceit that has walled us off from reality. And as He shows us faults within, rather than accuse ourselves or blame others, we must turn immediately to Him in confession. As we confess, the Spirit rushes in to cleanse us of the unrighteousness that our self-examination has revealed.

Practice immediate confession. When you become aware of some expression of sin in your life, don't wait. Confess it immediately, saying to God: "Lord, I have sinned in (*identify the specific sin*), and I confess it now to you." Then thank Him for His forgiveness and His cleansing. And go on with your life.

Don't be disturbed if the sin you confess recurs. Cleansing, like growth, is a process that takes time. An ugly caterpillar doesn't become a beautiful butterfly overnight; a field of corn never is harvested the day after planting. However, we can be sure that as we practice confession, we open our lives to God's loving work and to *growth* toward holiness.

TO THINK ABOUT AND DO

1. Read the story of the Prodigal Son (Luke 15:11–25). If this were your personal story, where have you "departed" from your Father's house? What emotions did you feel in leaving? Have you sensed the emptiness of the far country? In your imagination, return to the Father. Rehearse, as the son did, the confession you will make. Then experience the Father's joyous welcome; feel in your own soul the cleansing flow of divine forgiveness.

2. In your time alone with God, ask Him to reveal areas of sin in your life. Listen quietly. Don't worry that God will overwhelm you by showing you all your sins at one time; He will gently reveal them one by one.

   As you become aware of God's presence, picture Christ dying for your sins—the very sins God is revealing to you. Then place the burden of your sins at the foot of the cross. Say to God, "Lord, I surrender to you my pride (or anger or bitterness or jealousy or dishonesty or self-indulgence). I am sorry for my sin. Please forgive me." Then hear Him say to you, "My Son died for your sins. I forgive you in His name." For a week, keep a diary of your discoveries and experiences.

3. Read a good book about forgiveness, like Bruce Narramore's *No Condemnation: Rethinking Guilt Motivation in Counseling, Preaching, and Parenting* (Grand Rapids: Zondervan Publishing House, 1984).

4. Select several verses to memorize. Tell someone why you selected these particular verses and what you hope memorizing them will do for you.

4

RESPONSIBILITY

"I want you to listen to a story and make a judgment. Last week a twenty-year-old man shot his wife and two children, then he aimed the gun at his head and killed himself. The police found the room littered with liquor bottles. The neighbors say that the woman had called the police often when her husband had beat her. The man also had been arrested several times for drunk driving. Now, tell me, on a scale from 0% to 100%, how responsible was the man?"

"100%."

"At least 70%."

"About 90%."

"OK. Who do courts and others say is responsible for the other percent?"

"Oh, parents, unhappy childhood, immaturity, lack of educational opportunity, traumatic experiences, rejection. All sorts of things."

It was an interesting discussion. We all agreed that the person who takes the action is primarily responsible. But when we started to look at ourselves, we had questions. When we do something we know is wrong, who is really responsible? Does someone "make" us mad or are we responsible for any anger we feel? When a friend asks us to twist the truth to protect him or her, is the friend responsible for the white lie we tell or are we responsible? When we constantly criticize others, are we responsible or are the critical parents who gave us negative role models responsible?

Eden Revisited

When God created human beings, He created them in the "image" and "likeness" of the Godhead (Gen. 1:26a). The Hebrew words found here are *selem* and *demût*, words used only in contexts where the Old Testament is making some affirmation about human nature (see also Gen. 1; 2; 5:1, 3). *Selem* means "image" or "representation," while *demût,* a word of comparison, is translated "likeness." Together they comprise the technical, theological term *image-likeness,* which affirms that even though God can't be understood by comparing Him to any created thing, human nature can be understood only by comparing it to God. Image-likeness indentifies you and me as unique and reminds us that every person is so special, so precious that nothing could ever be offered to compensate for the loss of a single human life (see also Gen. 9:5–6).†

Our human image-likeness to God's nature has many implications. Like God, we humans are fully *persons.* We have emotions and intellect. We have a will, and we can make choices. We can appreciate beauty and exercise creativity. We can do meaningful work. We need and can enjoy relationships with other persons, and with God Himself. Ours is a proud and very special calling.

We are persons. We have been made in the image and likeness of our God. Yet, when sin entered, this image was marred. Emotions were twisted so that we sometimes desire what is wrong. The intellect was darkened so that sometimes we view what is wrong as good. And the will was crippled, so that our choices all too often fail to reflect godliness. But while the image-likeness of God was distorted, it is still present in us (see Gen. 9:6; James 3:9). We remain persons. We remain beings who can be truly understood only when we compare who and what we are to God.

One of the first evidences of sin in the Garden was Adam and Eve's refusal to admit their responsibility. When God found the guilty pair, He asked them, "Have

†See introduction to Section A, p. 73.

you eaten from the tree that I commanded you not to eat from?" (Gen. 3:11b).

Too quickly Adam responded. "Uh, the woman you put here with me—well, she gave me some fruit from the tree and, uh, well, I guess I did eat it." This response shows clearly that sin had worked death in Adam's once vital and spotless personality. For in seeking to blame God (the woman *you* put here with me) and in seeking to make Eve responsible (*she* gave me some fruit), Adam had denied himself.

Adam claimed that God (that is, the circumstances of his life as God had shaped them) or Eve (that is, the influence of another person) had determined his choice. In making this claim, Adam denied that he was what God had made him, a person in his own right, whose very personhood implies personal responsibility for his acts. *In denying responsibility, Adam had denied his essential personhood—and thus his likeness to God.*

Bondage

Ever since Adam's fall, we all have been aware of our sin. We know what it means to fall short of our own standards, much less God's. And we don't like that feeling. As we discussed in the last chapter, we often blame other people rather than face our own sin.

"It's his fault."

"My father abused me."

"Circumstances are to blame."

"What else could you expect from someone who has been through what I have?"

All these excuses come easily to our lips, because we human beings tend to see personal responsibility as personal bondage. We think, "If I am really responsible, then I am trapped!"

The Old Testament addresses this fear of responsibility.† Ezekiel wrote to a generation that saw the coming judgment of God on Jerusalem and that shrugged it off by saying: "The fathers eat sour grapes, and the children's teeth are set on edge" (Ezek. 18:2). Today we might say, Our parents sucked lemons, and we puckered. What the saying means, of course, is that what happens to me is my parents' fault. There's nothing I can do. My present is *determined* by what was done *to me* by others in the past.

This reasoning is still popular. Do I lack motivation and self-discipline? It must be my mother's fault for making my bed for me instead of teaching me to do it myself. Does he steal? Well, it must be society's fault for not helping him get a job. Do you have heart trouble? It can't be because you are a hundred pounds overweight.

Now, certainly unwise mothers and social inequities do influence our lives. But these do not determine our choices or our future. And this was the message Ezekiel had for people of his time. You are human beings! You have been given the gift of personal responsibility. And nothing can rob you of that heritage!

And so Ezekiel announced that "the soul who sins is the one who will die" (Ezek. 18:4b). He told the people that when the Babylonians would sweep away Jerusalem's last defenses and when the blood would run deep in the streets of the Holy City, the people who would die would be those who had sinned. God would make a distinction, even in the crush and uncertainty of war, between the good person and the evil person. And God promised through His prophet that, in that particular invasion, the righteous would survive.

In making this announcement, Ezekiel went on to stress again and again that each person would be judged on the basis of his or her own acts. The evil son of a good father would die: his father's righteousness would not save him.

†This discussion is based on chapter 6, p. 78.

The good son of an evil father would live: his father's wickedness would not destroy him. And even a wicked person who "turns away from all the sins he has committed and keeps all my decrees and does what is just and right, he will surely live" (Ezek. 18:21). And in this last statement, Ezekiel affirms a wonderful truth. *Even a person's own past actions do not determine what he or she will do in the future.* Each human being has been given the gift of personal responsibility. And each of us can accept responsibility for our own acts. We are free to change!

The Bible's affirmation of individual personal responsibility is not a message of bondage but a word of freedom!

Jesus and Responsibility†

As we look into the New Testament, we see that Jesus too had a message of personal responsibility. He taught that we never can shift responsibility for our acts to someone else. Thus He reminded us that we "will have to give account on the day of judgment for every careless word [we] have spoken" (Matt. 12:36). The Epistles also teach that we will need to give account, for a day of judgment has been set (see Rom. 14:12; Heb. 4:13; 13:17; 1 Peter 4:5). While Christians cannot be judged for sins, for these have been paid for by Jesus and are washed away, you and I will need to give an account of our stewardship as a basis for heavenly rewards.

Still, what is most striking in the Gospels is the fact that Jesus Himself was a responsible human being. He modeled for us what personal responsibility means. And Jesus shows us just what we are responsible *for!*

We hear it echoed in His words, "I do nothing on my own but speak just what the Father has taught me" (John 8:28b). Jesus lived in perfect unity with the Father, who never left Jesus alone, "for I always do what pleases him"

†This discussion is based on chapter 6, pp. 78–80.

(John 8:29b). Jesus was responsible to do His Father's will, to speak His Father's words, to reflect His Father's nature.

Doing God's will in no way robbed Jesus of His freedom, which we see most clearly in the choice that led Christ to the Cross. Even there He said, "No one takes [my life] from me, but I lay it down of my own accord. I have *authority* to lay it down and *authority* to take it up again. This command I received from my Father" (John 10:18, italics added).

It is in these last words that we discover both the title deed to our own freedom and a vital key to living our human life in touch with God. The Greek word rendered "authority" is *exousia*. While the word has a wide range of meaning, each reflects a central, basic concept: "freedom of choice." The greater the *exousia*, the greater the extent of unrestricted freedom of action. A person with little *exousia* had little freedom of action, for others with greater *exousia* had the power to limit that person's freedom. Thus, for instance, an army private has less freedom of action than a sergeant, who has less freedom of action than a lieutenant, who has less freedom than a colonel, etc. Each higher rank has the freedom to command and thus to limit the freedom of those people in lower ranks.

The question is, then, what authority—what freedom of action—did Jesus claim? *Jesus claimed the freedom to obey God within the context of His personal circumstances and calling.* Jesus claimed freedom to obey God, even to laying down and taking up His life again, because He received "this command . . . from [His] Father" (John 10:18b).

The Bible's view of human responsibility is closely linked with its teaching on *exousia;* that is, with its teaching on personal freedom of action. On the one hand, Scripture recognizes that we all live in different circumstances. In New Testament times some people were slaves, some masters; some were Jews, some Gentiles;

some were male, some female; some were learned, some unlearned. Today we too live in differing circumstances: some of us are married, some single; some are wealthy, some poor; some of us had Christian parents, some unbelieving parents; some have jobs, some are unemployed; some live in cities, some in small towns. We have different temperaments, different callings, different gifts, different occupations. To some degree, our circumstances limit the range of choices open to us. A poor person in the modern world can't choose to fly to some exotic location for a vacation: A person who lives on a farm can't take classes at a metropolitan art museum. Restrictions like these always have existed and always will exist. But such restrictions are irrelevant to the issue of freedom and responsibility!

The freedom of the Christian always has been nothing more and nothing less than freedom to obey God within the framework of his or her personal circumstances and calling. The fact that my circumstances limit the choices I can make does nothing to change the fact that, within the limitations of my situation, I have the authority (*exousia*) to make the choices available to me by the will of God!

The person who lives his or her life in touch with God, then, will take both responsibility and freedom to heart. The spiritual person recognizes that his or her choices are not determined by circumstances, by others, or even by past choices. No one and nothing can be blamed when we make choices we know are wrong. But the spiritual person also realizes that he or she *does not have* to make wrong choices! We each have the authority, that amazing freedom of action implied by *exousia,* to make the choices available to us by the will of God!

To live our human life in touch with God and in union with Him means that we accept responsibility for our actions and that we make our choices according to what we understand to be the will of God.

Claiming our Freedom

The Bible's message of personal responsibility is a promise of true freedom. We are not bound. We can make our choices, as Jesus did, by the will of God. But how do we claim our freedom and grow as responsible persons?

Take charge. Many of us live fantasy lives or drift along doing things by habit. For instance, sometimes we fantasize about what it would be like to have a different job. We imagine that we would be so much happier, so much more effective if only we had a different work situation. Maybe we even imagine that we could be a better person—a better spouse, a better church member, a better steward—if only we had a different job. But this is fantasy. What we need to consider is not what we would do if we had another job, but what God wants us to do with the job we have now.

The Christian life can't be constructed on the "if onlys" and the "might have beens." We have to deal with the reality of who and where we are, and we need to decide to do God's will in our present circumstances.

It's much the same with habit. When we come home from work, do we drop down to spend the evening in front of the TV? Is it our habit to have dessert with every meal? Is it habit to mock other people with our humor? Is it habit to yell at our children rather than take the time to talk through a problem? Is it habit to let someone else do the work on church committees? Is it habit to ride the elevator instead of walking up one or two flights of stairs? Some of these things are not necessarily wrong in themselves. The problem is that our habits often are unexamined areas of our lives. We need to stop and ask ourselves, Do I do this or that because it is the best choice I can make? Is it God's will for me to do this particular thing? By looking at the unexamined areas of our lives, we may discover exciting new ways to be God's person, to be responsible for our choices.

Taking charge of our lives means not only realizing that our choices are significant but also choosing what is in harmony with God's will. Taking charge of our lives means making decisions that will help us say, "I do this because it pleases God."

Stay alert. We need to stay alert to the self-deceit we often practice. When we become aware of our own sin and failures, we often excuse ourselves by blaming someone or something else. But when we begin to think this way, we become like Adam—we deny our personhood. God made us responsible beings, and we have no valid excuse for our wrong choices. So we need to stay alert for the deceptive thoughts and half-wishes that can corrupt us. And when we recognize them, we must decisively reject them. When we make a wrong choice, we need to say—to others and to ourselves—"I am responsible." The more we assume responsibility for our actions, the more we will be able to claim our freedom and consciously make the right choice next time.

Commit to God's will. Finally, like Jesus, we need to commit ourselves to do the will of God as we understand it. The true freedom of the Christian is the freedom to do God's will. When we have finally accepted the fact that we are responsible beings and when we are in touch with that reality, we will see many opportunities to respond to God. When we stop living by habit, abandon fantasy, and see ourselves as fully responsible for the choices we make each day, we can consciously submit ourselves to the Lord and expect Him to show us fresh and exciting ways to please Him.

TO THINK ABOUT AND DO

1. Make a list of the things you do each day, from when you wake up to when you go to bed. Then look at it

carefully. Which actions are done out of habit? Are they good habits or bad habits? If you find a bad habit, what are you willing to do about it? How will a change in this habit change your life? What alternative uses of your time or resources can you choose?

2. Compare your list with the other people's lists. Talk about the patterns you see in your lives. Are you satisfied with them? Why or why not? What are you prepared to do about it?

3. What choices that you make are influenced more by other people than by what you think is best? List these choices and compare them to what you think God's will is for each choice. How can you bring your decisions into harmony with God's will? Ask a friend to pray with you about these decisions.

4. Draw a picture of a cage. On each bar of the cage, write some event, circumstance, or person that you think has influenced your choices. Then study Ezekiel 18:1–29. What does its teaching suggest that you do with the bars?

5. During your prayer time with God, submit to Him your bad habits and the "bars of your cage." First, close your eyes and meditate about God's greatness and His love for you. Next, picture Jesus, dying on the cross for your sins and bad habits. Then picture Jesus sitting across from you with His hand stretched out in front of you. One by one place each of your bad habits into His open hand, saying, "Lord, I give you (name a specific bad habit). What is Your will for me? (Be silent, waiting for the Lord to prompt you with a Scripture verse or a sense of direction.) Help me to do Your will." Then give Him each bar in your cage, saying, "Lord, I submit to you (name a specific bar of your cage). I choose to take responsibility for my actions. Help me, Lord."

5

GOD'S WILL

"It's all right to talk about responsibility and doing God's will. But I noticed you said doing 'what you understand to be' God's will."

"That's right. You did."

"So, how do we know what God's will is?"

"I remember when we once ignored God's inner urgings," said Karen. *"Years ago, when my husband was in graduate school, our car broke down. We needed to buy another one, but since we couldn't afford much, we looked for a used car. We saw a Renault that wasn't very expensive. Although neither of us felt completely positive about the car, we felt the urgency of needing to replace our other one. We took a walk to pray about the decision, asking God to show us if this was the right car to buy. When it came time to sign the papers, I felt reluctant, but I brushed it off as my own indecision. I later realized that my reluctance was God's way of telling us no. Three months later the Renault broke down and needed major repairs that were more than the value of the car. We had bought the wrong car. And what's more, God had revealed His will to us, but we were too immature to recognize it or too unwilling to follow it."*

Many of us have had experiences like Karen's. We sense an inner direction in our lives, but we're not sure if it is God or our own thoughts that urge us in one direction or another. We want to do God's will, but we're not sure how to discern His voice.

To live a human life in union with God means to become increasingly aware of His presence with us and of His voice leading us. First, how do we know that God is present with us? How do we learn to sense His presence with us in our everyday experiences? I suggest we look at what God says about Himself in Scripture, specifically what He says about His name "Lord."

"Lord" in Scripture†

The Old Testament. In the Old Testament the word most often rendered "LORD" (note the use of small capital letters for this term) is the name Yahweh. Most scholars believe that this name, formed from the four Hebrew consonants YHWH, is derived from the Hebrew verb "to be" or "to become." The word emphasizes existence God told Moses, tell the people my name is "I AM" (Exod. 3:14).

The context in which this name of God was first introduced is important. Moses, who had dreamed as a youth of delivering Israel from Egypt, had for forty years been nothing but a shepherd in political isolation. Then suddenly God appeared to him in a burning bush and commissioned him to return to Egypt and accomplish the mission he had dreamed of.

But Moses hesitated and tried to convince God he was not the man for the job. Finally Moses said to God,

> "Suppose I go to the Israelites and say to them, 'The God of your fathers has sent me to you,' and they ask me, 'What is his name?' Then what shall I tell them?"
>
> God said to Moses, "I AM WHO I AM. This is what you are to say to the Israelites: 'I AM has sent me to you.'"
>
> God also said to Moses, ". . . This is my name forever, the name by which I am to be remembered from generation to generation" (Exod. 3:13–14, 15b).

Later the Lord told Moses more about His name. He spoke of His earlier appearances to Abraham, Isaac, and Jacob as God Almighty. But, He said, "by my name the LORD I did not make myself known to them" (Exod. 6:3b).

There was something special about the name LORD. Something so special that, for all time, God wants His

---

†This discussion is based on chapter 12, pp. 154–156.

people to identify Him first by this name. What is so special? And why was the time of Moses the critical time for introducing the name?

Moses was returning to Egypt to a people who had lived for generations as slaves. These people had heard of God. They had heard the stories about how God appeared to Abraham and made wonderful promises. They probably had dreamed about a future when those promises would be kept. But they knew only slavery. Their God might have been real in the past—to Abraham. He might be real in the future—to the fortunate final generation. But He didn't seem very real to them!

And then Moses came, a solitary figure from the desert. With Moses came a sudden, terrifying outburst of miracles. The God whom they had heard about was suddenly *there!* He was present, turning the Nile waters to blood. He was present, bringing hordes of frogs and clouds of lice and locusts. He was there in the hail that destroyed Egypt's crops and livestock. He was there in a darkness so dense they could feel it. God was there in the death of Egypt's firstborn. He was powerfully present in the parting of the sea. He was visibly present in the fiery/cloudy pillar that stood above the camp.

God in His mighty acts demonstrated the appropriateness of His name. God showed Himself to be the I AM—the one who is always present!

This is the real meaning of the Old Testament's name, Yahweh, the name we read as LORD. It means that God *is*. God is not limited to the past or limited to the future, but He is present with us now, and He will be present with His people forever.

The New Testament. The Greek word that the New Testament translates "lord" is *kurios*. In ordinary speech it was a term of respect, much like our word "sir" or an earlier "master." It was typically used by a person addressing a superior.

But when the Old Testament was translated into Greek, the word *kurios* was used to represent the Hebrew YHWH, "LORD." And while at times Jesus was addressed as "lord" in the cultural meaning of "master" (see Matt. 8:2; Luke 9:59b), Jesus Himself used "Lord" to identify Himself with Deity (see Matt. 12:8; Luke 20:42–44). And the disciples also used it in this same way at various times (see John 20:28).

After the resurrection, the Christian church immediately began to confess that "Jesus is Lord." Acts, and the rest of the New Testament, affirms Jesus' lordship in the very fullest sense. *To say that "Jesus is Lord" is both to affirm that He is the Yahweh of the Old Testament and to affirm that Jesus Himself is present with us now!*

As we look through the New Testament we see even more clearly the meaning of Christ's lordship. As Lord, Jesus has universal authority (Eph. 1:21). Every natural and supernatural power is subject to Him (1 Peter 3:22). He is sovereign in this present world. We can view every experience as an expression of His Lordship, and we can be confident that He is actively superintending the events of our lives (1 Peter 3:12, 15). As Lord, Jesus claims personal authority over every believer (Rom. 14:9). As "head over everything for the church," He claims to be actively involved in directing the life of the body (Eph. 1:22b).

Living a human life in union with God means recognizing His lordship: His presence with us and His authority over us. But how are we to respond to that presence and that authority over us? Again we look to our model, Jesus. We can look at how He responded to His Father.

Jesus and His Father's Voice

Jesus gives us a clear example of how we can acknowlededge God's presence with us and listen to His voice. Jesus teaches us two things: the God who is present with us will speak to us, and when He does, we are to respond in obedience.

Jesus spoke of His relationship to His Father in words we looked at earlier:

> I tell you the truth, the Son can do nothing by himself; he can do only what he sees his Father doing, because whatever the Father does the Son also does. For the Father loves the Son and shows him all he does (John 5:19–20a).

> I do nothing on my own but speak just what the Father has taught me. The one who sent me is with me; he has not left me alone, for I always do what pleases him (John 8:28c–29).

Jesus' teaching did more than affirm His special relationship to His Father. Jesus also taught that we can have a similar relationship to Him! Jesus promised that "anyone who has faith in me will do what I have been doing" (John 14:12a).

Jesus knew the will of God, for in the intimacy of their relationship, the Father communicated His will to His Son. Jesus said that the one who was *with Him* showed Him what to do. That same God is present with us, and in the intimacy of our relationship, He will show us what to do.

This is the confidence we can have: God will show us what to do. We are bonded to Jesus by faith; we live in vital union with Him. And when we truly experience that vital union, we will hear the Father's voice speaking to us.

Christ not only teaches us that God will speak to us, but He also teaches us that we must submit to His voice. Christ's lordship was rooted in a paradox: His authority came from His submission. Philippians 2 describes this paradox. Although Jesus was "in very nature God," He willingly "made himself nothing, taking the very nature of a servant." Then, in human likeness, Jesus "humbled himself and became obedient to death—even the death on the cross" (Phil. 2:6–8).

The phrase "obedient to death" is more than an historical statement. It is a statement of the complete and total submission of Jesus, as He willingly obeyed God the Father.

The writer of the Book of Hebrews makes a similar observation. Jesus' prayer was heard because of His "reverent submission" and "although he was a son, he learned obedience from what he suffered" (Heb. 5:7c–8). Jesus' lordship flows from His life of submission on earth.

In His intimate relationship with the Father, Jesus had learned to hear His Father's voice. And He had determined that He would do whatever the Father asked Him to do or say. He lived in total submission to His Father's will.

Jesus taught His followers that they were to live in the same submission and obedience:

> Whoever has my commands and obeys them, he is the one who loves me. He who loves me will be loved by my Father, and I too will love him and show myself to him. . . . If anyone loves me, he will obey my teaching. My Father will love him, and we will come to him and make our home with him. He who does not love me will not obey my teaching. These words you hear are not my own; they belong to the Father who sent me (John 14:21, 23–24).

To live a human life in union with God means recognizing His voice and choosing to obey Him.

Hearing God's Voice†

In his letter to the Corinthians, Paul explains that it is the Spirit's work within us that enables us to discern the

†This discussion is based on chapter 12, pp. 157–159.

will of God. Then Paul makes a profound statement: "The spiritual man makes judgments about all things, but he himself is not subject to any man's judgment: 'For who has known the mind of the Lord that he may instruct him?' But *we have the mind of Christ*" (1 Cor. 2:15–16, italics added).

Because Jesus is Lord, truly the one who is present, and because we have the Spirit within us, we *can* know the mind of Christ and respond to God with obedience.

Let's look at how the writer addresses this issue in Hebrews 3:7–4:13. As we trace through the passage, we discover a principle that teaches us how to experience Jesus' lordship in our own life and how to discern the present will of God.

The writer looks back on Moses' time, when the first generation after the Exodus was poised on the edge of the Promised Land. There they heard God's voice commanding them to enter. But that generation was afflicted with a "sinful, unbelieving heart." They refused to obey—and their bodies later were buried in the wilderness.

So the writer warns us, quoting from Psalm 95,

"Today, if you hear his voice,
    do not harden your hearts
as you did in the rebellion" (Heb. 3:15).

That warning is appropriate for us too. Today—this very day—if we hear His voice, we must not harden our hearts. How often have we heard the voice of God but haven't listened because of our hardened hearts? How often have we consciously or unconsciously ignored His voice?

The real question facing us is not, What can I do? The real issue facing us is, Will I submit to God and let Him guide me into His solution?

"So when I felt that inner nudge that said 'Don't buy this car,' I should have listened to it and trusted God."

61

"Yes, but are we supposed to go by feelings? How can you tell whether that feeling is God or some bad meat you had the night before?"

"That's right. And how does Scripture fit in? Aren't we supposed to have everything we need to guide us in the Bible?"

Many people are uncomfortable with the idea that God has a contemporary voice that speaks directly to the believer. It sounds too much like some "inner light" that replaces the objective truth of Scripture. But the fact is that the contemporary voice of God operates in harmony with Scripture.

After all, the God who insists that He be known as LORD throughout every generation, the one who is always present with His people, is the God who inspired the Scripture! We would hardly expect God to contradict Himself, saying one thing in the Word and another within us.

The written Word is authoritative. It provides us with an objective check on our subjective judgments. God will never lead us to do something Scripture forbids.

The written Word is also sanctifying (John 17:17). As we saturate ourselves in Scripture, God reshapes our perspectives. We come to understand the issues of life from His point of view, and we gradually test our values and motives. So study of the Bible makes us more sensitive to God, more likely to hear and to recognize His voice when He speaks to us.

This makes study of the Bible particularly important as we seek to grow spiritually. We need to understand the principles and precepts of the Word of God to better recognize God's voice. Jesus taught that one of the ministries of the Holy Spirit is to "teach you all things and . . . remind you of everything I have said to you" (John 14:26). The Word needs to be in our minds and hearts for the Spirit to do His "reminding" work.

Having said all this, we must realize that the Bible does

not cover every situation. For instance, should we take this job or that one? On what Christian ministry should we focus financial support? Is this the right time to buy a home? When should we break off that relationship or step into a new one? Each of us faces dozens of decisions like these. And for these decisions there is no clear and simple verse that tells us, "Thus says the Lord." Karen could hardly turn to 1 Corinthians and find a verse that said, "Don't buy that car!"

What is exciting, though, is that while Scripture is not *intended* to give this kind of specific direction, we have a personal relationship with a living God who is with us! When we are facing a decision for which we need special guidance, we can turn to Him, and we can confidently expect to hear—and recognize—His voice.

Doing God's Will

What are some practical ways we can keep in touch with God's voice and His will?

Read the Word. Daily spend time in the Word of God, reading to learn more about what God is like and what is important to Him. The better we understand God's thinking, His motives, His ways, the more sensitive we can be to His will.

Recognize His voice. God does not speak to His people in one particular way. Sometimes we will hear His voice in a verse of Scripture. Sometimes He will speak to us through a friend's advice. I once heard God's voice speaking through a billboard in front of a Christian radio station. At times there will be no external avenue through which God speaks: you will simply become aware that God does or doesn't want you to do a particular thing.

But Jesus said something that is very important for us to remember. He said that His sheep follow Him because they *know* His voice (John 10:4)! We can be sure that when Jesus does speak to us, we who are His sheep will recognize His voice.

Keep a sensitive heart. If our hearts are hard, we will not listen to God, even if we hear His voice. We must learn to keep our hearts soft, sensitive to the Father's voice. Commit yourself daily to listening to—not just to hearing—the Lord's voice.

The Hebrews passage says "Today, *if* you should hear his voice." That "if" is important. Sometimes we won't hear the Father's voice, even though we are straining to hear it. God has made us responsible beings, and sometimes He will want us to make the choice ourselves. When the voice is silent, we need to act responsibly, making the best decisions we can.

It may be helpful to imagine that God's voice operates like an airliner's flight-path indicator. It's only when the aircraft strays from the right path that the electronic "beep, beep" warns the pilot. As we live on course with God, acting on His will as we understand it, unusual guidance seldom may be necessary.

Obey. This is a very important point. Our sensitivity to God's presence with us grows only as we respond to Him in obedience. This is how we express love for the Lord. And this is how love opens our heart to become more and more aware of His presence.

So probably the single most important thing we can do to be in touch with the Lord's will is determine to obey Him now. We can ask each morning, Lord, what do you want me to do? And we can be careful to take those little, daily steps of obedience even in things that may seem unimportant. For as we do, our awareness of God's presence, our love for Him, and our responsiveness to His voice all will grow.

TO THINK ABOUT AND DO

1. Is there anything you do regularly because you are aware that God wants you to do it? What is it? Tell at least one other person about it.

2. In your time alone with God, meditate about His promises to guide you. Think about areas in your life that need His wisdom and guidance. Then pray, committing those areas to His lordship. Ask God to reveal His will to you. Listen in silence. Tell God that you are prepared do what He tells you to do. If God does not reveal His answer to you during your quiet time together, listen for His answer during the week as you meditate on the Scriptures and as you talk to other believers. When He reveals His will, make sure you obey it completely.

3. Read a chapter of Scripture (a chapter from one of the Epistles, for instance) with several other people. As you read, write answers to these two questions: What does this tell me about God and what is important to Him? What does this tell me about what God wants me to do?

   Share your answers with each other. Then discuss: How might this approach to reading the Bible help us grow in our experience of Jesus' lordship? How can we put into practice *this week* what God wants us to do?

4. In a sense, a person's "lord" is whoever or whatever he or she looks to for guidance in determining decisions. Some people make money (the "bottom line") the basis for their decisions: Will I turn a profit? Some make other people lord: What will he or she think?

   List the "lords" that tend to affect daily decisions of Christian people. Evaluate: If Jesus were to be the only Lord in my life, would my decisions be different? Which decisions? How would they be different?

6

ACCEPTANCE

"I'd like you to respond to a series of remarks. As you hear them, think about what you hear. These are remarks any of us could have made."

"How can they afford that new car? I know they have trouble buying groceries."

"I thought she dedicated her life to mission work at a recent conference. Her new job as an accountant is hardly missionary work."

"I think his sleeping late is just irresponsible. He's got to learn to get up early and get to work."

"Look, they deserve this trouble. How could they expect to raise a family on his income as a sculptor? He should have gotten a real job years ago."

Well, our group heard many different things. For the most part, they agreed with the remarks. Feeding your family comes before new cars. A person who makes a vow should keep it. It is irresponsible to sleep late when there's work to do. And if people don't make good decisions, sooner or later they will have to pay for their poor choices. But some of us "heard" something more.

We heard in the remarks a subtle tone that doesn't fit with what the Bible teaches about the lordship of Jesus. We heard judgment.

Our group studied several Scripture verses to see what the Bible says about judging others. One of the verses is a verse we examined in the last chapter. Because the person who lives by the Spirit has access to the mind of Christ, that person can "make judgments about all things, but he himself is not subject to any man's judgment" (1 Cor. 2:15). Because our union with Jesus is real, each of us can hear and follow God's voice.

The second verse is something of a corollary. The

people in Corinth had been very critical of the apostle Paul. So in his first letter to them, Paul reminds them that he is a "servant of Christ," and says,

> Now it is required that those who have been given a trust must prove faithful. I care very little if I am judged by you or by any human court; indeed, I do not even judge myself. My conscience is clear, but that does not make me innocent. It is the Lord who judges me. Therefore judge nothing before the appointed time; wait till the Lord comes. He will bring to light what is hidden in darkness and will expose the motives of men's hearts. At that time each will receive praise from God (1 Cor. 4:2–5).

See it? Paul argues that no human court is competent to judge any person: we can't even judge ourselves accurately. Jesus, who is Lord, will come. And at that time He will expose what is hidden to mere humanity, for it is "the Lord who judges." Recognizing our lack of competence to see into the heart and motives of another person, we are to withhold judgment. The Lord is judge.

Judgment is an aspect of Christ's lordship, and we must acknowledge His lordship by resisting the temptation to judge others. To live a human life in union with God means to allow Him to judge. We must submit our judgmental attitudes to Him, trusting Him to lead the person we are judging.

Acceptance†

It is in the context of this aspect of Jesus' lordship that the New Testament introduces its teaching on accepting one another. In the context of lordship, "acceptance" simply means to welcome into fellowship all brothers and sisters in the Lord, without considering our differences from them in matters that are disputable.

†This discussion is based on chapter 13, pp. 164–167.

The phrase "matters that are disputable" is important. We should not accept differences in matters that Scripture clearly identifies as sin. That is rightly a matter for church discipline. However, in 99% of the differences that divide Christians or that stimulate us to judge each other, sin is not an issue. Instead, the differences are in areas that are "disputable"—that is, areas in which we have no clear "thou shalt not" in the Word of God.

Paul deals rather extensively with this issue in Romans. Although it's a long passage, read it carefully and underline the significant phrases. Remember, the issue is judging others in disputable matters. And the theological key is the reality of Jesus' lordship in His relationship to each person who is bonded to Him through personal faith.

> Accept him whose faith is weak, without passing judgment on disputable matters. One man's faith allows him to eat everything, but another man, whose faith is weak, eats only vegetables. The man who eats everything must not look down on him who does not, and the man who does not eat everything must not condemn the man who does, for God has accepted him. Who are you to judge someone else's servant? To his own master he stands or falls. And he will stand, for the Lord is able to make him stand.

> One man considers one day more sacred than another; another man considers every day alike. Each one should be fully convinced in his own mind. He who regards one day as special, does so to the Lord. He who eats meat, eats to the Lord, for he gives thanks to God; and he who abstains, does so to the Lord and gives thanks to God. For none of us lives to himself alone and none of us dies to himself alone. If we live, we live to the Lord; and if we die, we die to the Lord. So, whether we live or die, we belong to the Lord.

> For this very reason, Christ died and returned to life so that he might be the Lord of both the dead and the living.

You, then, why do you judge your brother? Or why do you look down on your brother? For we will all stand before God's judgment seat (Rom. 14:1–10).

Therefore let us stop passing judgment on one another. Instead, make up your mind not to put any stumbling block or obstacle in your brother's way. As one who is in the Lord Jesus, I am fully convinced that no food is unclean in itself. But if anyone regards something as unclean, then for him it is unclean. If your brother is distressed because of what you eat, you are no longer acting in love (Rom. 14:13–15).

So whatever you believe about these things keep between yourself and God. Blessed is the man who does not condemn himself by what he approves. But the man who has doubts is condemned if he eats, because his eating is not from faith; and everything that does not come from faith is sin (Rom. 14:22–23).

Accept one another, then, just as Christ accepted you, in order to bring praise to God (Rom. 15:7).

Let me list a few of the key points made in this passage. If you didn't underline them just now, go back and make sure just where these teachings are found.

1. "Passing judgment" is expressed by *looking down on* or by *condemning* others.

2. As God's servants, we are responsible only to Jesus for our convictions about "disputable matters."

3. We are to make choices in these matters as a conscious response to Christ as Lord, acting as we are "fully convinced in [our] own mind[s]."

4. While we are not to judge others in life's disputable matters, we are to be sensitive to their convictions and show sensitivity in our own choices.

5. We never are to make an issue of our convictions in disputable matters; our personal response to Jesus' lordship is between us and Him, and our convictions are not to be imposed on others.

6. We are to accept our brothers and sisters as freely as Jesus has accepted us. We are not to judge them, but we are to allow them to be responsible—and responsive—to Jesus as Lord.

Jesus and Acceptance†

A number of Jesus' teachings recorded in the Gospels lay a foundation for Paul's extended explanation in the Book of Romans. Jesus said "Do not judge, or you too will be judged. For in the same way you judge others, you will be judged, and with the measure you use, it will be measured to you" (Matt. 7:1–2). In this statement Jesus warns us that if we begin to judge our brothers and sisters, others will soon judge us. Christians should be known for their love, not for their criticisms and bickering. But if we accept each other rather than judge and criticize, we contribute to the spirit of unity that permits us "with one heart and mouth" to "glorify the God and Father of our Lord Jesus Christ" (Rom. 15:6).

Two additional passages in John's gospel are significant. John 5 quotes Jesus' claim of authority to judge. This authority was granted by God the Father, for the Father "has entrusted *all judgment* to the Son" (John 5:22b, italics added). John 8 helps us understand why this must be. Jesus told the religious rulers who claimed the right of judgment in Israel, "You judge by human standards." Only Christ, who knows the heart, is able to make right determinations (John 8:15a). We human beings are simply

†This discussion is based on chapter 13, pp. 167–168.

too limited by our own nature to be able to make accurate judgments about others.

Jesus is Lord. He not only claims the sole right to judge, but He specifically commands us *not to judge* others.

An encounter between Peter and Jesus illustrates the Lord's teaching about judging others. Peter had denied Jesus. Then, after the resurrection, Jesus called Peter aside and asked him three times, "Do you love me?"

Three times the shame-filled Peter responded, almost in a whisper: "Lord, you know that I love you." We can imagine Jesus nodding agreement to each answer. Jesus knew that Peter did love Him.

Still, three times Jesus asked. And with each of Peter's answers, Jesus reaffirmed His commission to Peter: "Feed my lambs; care for my sheep." Finally Jesus went on to predict that Peter's love one day would lead him to the very death he had been unwilling to face on the eve of Jesus' crucifixion.

It was then that Peter, still flustered, saw John standing near them and asked, "Lord, what about him?"

Jesus said, "If I want him to remain alive until I return, what is that to you? You must follow me" (John 21:15–23).

How often you and I merit that same rebuke. We look at others, we're disturbed by their choices, and we think or say "What about them?" "Jesus, do you really want *that* for them?" "Jesus, they should see things the way you've shown them to *me!*"

Christ's answer remains the same. "What is that to you? You must follow me." We are to concentrate not on others' response to Christ's lordship but on our own. What Christ asks of us may not be what He asks of someone else. What is "right" behavior for us in a disputable matter may not be "right" for another person. What matters is that each person looks to God for guidance about his or her behavior in a specific matter. Each of us must look to God for His individual leading.

Judging Others

Judging others is destructive not only to our own spiritual life, but also to the spiritual vitality of the body of Christ. We look at others and see what they do, and almost without conscious thought, we impose our standards, our values, and our convictions on them.

The trouble is, we aren't competent to judge. And even if we are right in our evaluations, we're wrong to judge.

Think back to the series of remarks our Bible study evaluated. What about the financially troubled family with the new car? It seems like such a poor use of the little money they have, and someone questioned their priorities. But just suppose that the wife's parents gave them the car. Maybe the financially troubled family didn't buy the car with their own money. We can't judge that.

Suppose the young accountant feels God led her to get experience in accounting—possibly as necessary background to her future mission work or perhaps the accounting firm *may be* her mission field.

Suppose the person who sleeps late is a "night person" who works late on personal projects that may not be highly visible but are important to him or her. Perhaps the quietness of the night is the only time the person can write without being interrupted by phones and family.

Suppose the decision to work as a sculptor was a response to a call—an act of obedience to God that carried a high personal and family cost.

Maybe none of these suppositions is correct. Maybe the people are wrong in their decisions. Maybe they are immature, selfish, and not responsive to Jesus' lordship at all. But that's not the point. *Even if our judgments are "right," we are wrong to judge.*

We have no right to look down on others. We have no

right to condemn them. Jesus is Lord. Our brothers and sisters are *His* servants. It is to Jesus they are accountable. It is to Jesus they must stand or fall. And "the Lord is able to make [them] stand" (Rom. 14:4b).

So acknowledging Christ's lordship involves two responses: first, we acknowledge His lordship in our own lives and learn to hear and follow His voice; second, we acknowledge His lordship in the lives of our brothers and sisters, and rather than judge them in disputable matters, we simply accept and love them.

Growing in the Grace of Acceptance

As we live our human lives in union with God, we need to discipline ourselves not to judge. We need to replace judging others with acceptance and thus to affirm Jesus' lordship in His church. What can we do?

Acknowledge the fact that judging others is sin. We need to be sensitive to the condemning thought, to that insidious attitude that looks down on others. Don't try to rationalize or justify such thoughts. Don't argue within that you are "right." Instead, recognize sin as sin, confess it immediately to God, and let the Lord cleanse you from this way of thinking about and relating to others.

Don't make your personal convictions an issue. Each of us has not only the right but the duty to seek God's will for us in areas of "disputable things." How will we set our priorities and use our money? Will we or won't we take that social drink? Should we or shouldn't we go to all the services at our church? Is this right to wear? What limits will I set for my teenage children? As we seek to bring every significant thing in our life into harmony with God's will for us, we each need to remember that what I seek and find is God's will for *me*—not necessarily for everyone. So while we may share our convictions humbly, we are never to make an issue of them in our relationships with other Christians.

Acknowledge the debt of love we owe others. Paul stresses this in Romans 14. Each of us has to live with others who have convictions of their own and who are not yet mature enough to realize that a conviction may be right for them and at the same time not necessary for others. At times our sensitivity for others will lead us to limit our own freedom to live by our convictions. But we must remember that the conscience of the least mature in the Christian community is not to establish the conscience for all.

Accept other Christians despite differences. The Greek word rendered "accept" in Romans 14 is *proslambanō.* It is a relational term in the New Testament, meaning "actively to accept into one's society or circle of friends." Probably the closest word we have is "welcome." It is rich in warmth, rich in gladness as it reaches out to embrace others into full fellowship. This is the word Paul uses to urge us to "accept him whose faith is weak, without passing judgment on disputable matters" (Rom. 14:1). We are not simply "to put up with" those who differ from us. We are not simply to stop the habit of judging them. We are to reach out, to seek their company, opening our lives to them in friendship, bonding ourselves to them by love. Then, in a supernatural unity based not on "sameness" but on Christ, we will truly glorify God.

TO THINK ABOUT AND DO

1. With your group, make a list of behaviors that are "disputable matters." What are not disputable matters? How have you confused the two?

2. Paul says we pass judgment when we "condemn" someone or when we "look down on" them. As you examine your own heart, identify any person you may

be condemning or looking down on. Examine your relationships to people in your family, in your study group, at your work, at church, among your friends.

As you become aware of your bad attitude now or in the future, immediately confess it (however "right" you may be!) as sin, and ask the Lord to cleanse you, to change your attitude, and to help you "accept" (welcome) the other person.

3. Memorize Romans 14:1–15:7. Let God's Word saturate your heart as well as your thinking. Meditate on this passage regularly, allowing the Lord to make it part of your life.

7

FORGIVENESS

Martha was angry. Her husband was sleeping in again. For months now Ken had been avoiding his work. He spent his nights out with the guys. And when he came home after midnight, she could smell he had been drinking.

For a year now he had managed his own car repair shop, and business was finally good enough to support their family of four. But lately his behavior was costing them money. Customers had begun to complain. Ken didn't get his work done on time. He was losing business.

Ken's behavior also was costing them frustration in the family. He was rarely home, and when he was, he yelled at the girls and wanted to be left alone. He took no responsibility for work around the house. Martha was getting desperate. And she was getting bitter.

To live a human life in union with God means not only facing the reality of sin in our own lives, but also dealing with the sins of others. As a Christian, Martha not only had to deal with her own sin, but she also had to deal with the results of her husband's sin. Her husband had faults, and those faults were irritating. He wasn't a responsible husband and father. He was losing his business because of his behavior.

Like the rest of us, Martha's husband was a sinner. And sin, in ourselves and in others around us, is something with which every human being who seeks to live in union with God must learn to deal.

In chapter 3 we discussed how to deal with the reality of our own sin. We learned the need and power of confession, of admitting our sin to God. In this chapter we will examine how God responds to our confession of sin and how we should respond to the sins of other people around us.

Forgiveness†

When we confess our sin to God, He responds not with condemnation or punishment, but with forgiveness. He looks at our sin, never dismissing it as trivial, and forgives us. What does it mean that He forgives us?

The Bible carefully develops its teaching about forgiveness. In the Old Testament, several Hebrew words are linked with forgiveness. *Kāpar,* meaning "atonement," refers to the removal of sin or of ritual defilement. *Nā´sā'* means "lift up" or "take away." The Old Testament affirms that God can "take away" the sin that makes us guilty before Him (see Ps. 32:1–5). *Sālah* and its derivative words mean "forgive" or "pardon." This word group, used only of God's offer to pardon sinners (see Isa. 55:6–7), is linked with atoning sacrifices (see Lev. 4:20; 5:10; 6:7).

The New Testament uses three Greek words that are rendered "forgive" in our versions. *Aphiēmi* reflects the emphasis of *nā´sā',* and teaches us that God does not simply overlook our guilt but literally takes away our sin. Forgiven sin no longer exists. The related noun, *Aphesis,* has this same emphasis, expressing remission of sins. Forgiveness in this aspect of removal or remission of sins is linked in the New Testament with the blood of Christ. Jesus' death on Calvary paid for the sins we have committed.

The third Greek word, *charizomai,* is different from the others and means "to be gracious" or "to give freely." It is often used to describe either forgiveness within the Christian community or canceling a debt. This word does not suggest taking away sin. Instead, it reflects a deep sense of compassion for the weakness of others. These words help us to grasp the wonder and power of forgiveness.

†This discussion is based on chapter 11, pp. 135–138.

Experiencing God's forgiveness. God's forgiveness comes to us in Jesus. Acts reminds us that "all the prophets testify about [Jesus] that everyone who believes in him receives forgiveness of [their] sins through his name" (Acts 10:43). The New Testament letters also link forgiveness to the death of Jesus. "We have redemption through his blood, the forgiveness of sins, in accordance with the riches of God's grace" (Eph. 1:7; Col. 1:14).

This teaching is most clearly developed in the Book of Hebrews. There the writer looks back on biblical history. He explains that the animal sacrifices of the bygone era were only an inadequate foreshadowing of the one, ultimate sacrifice of Jesus.

Why were the sacrifices inadequate? Because they could only make a person outwardly clean. They covered sin, but they never could take away sin. The very fact that the Old Testament sacrifices had to be be repeated endlessly, year after year, served to remind the Israelites that they were not fully cleansed. Thus, they continued to feel guilty for their sins (Heb. 10:1–4).

But now "the blood of Christ, who through the eternal Spirit offered himself unblemished to God" brings us complete forgiveness (Heb. 9:14b). In Christ we are forgiven for all sin, for Jesus has by one sacrifice taken all our sins away. This forgiveness promises us not only release from our nagging sense of guilt but also release from sin's ability to distort our future! Jesus' forgiveness is so complete that we can find release from our past and power to commit ourselves to serving God.

This is what Hebrews affirms when it teaches that Jesus' sacrifice has, and will, "cleanse our consciences from acts that lead to death, so that we may serve the living God" (Heb. 9:14c). We need not live in our past: the past is gone. What we once did can no longer program our future actions. We can move on to righteous living for "we have been made holy through the sacrifice of the body of Jesus Christ once for all" (Heb. 10:10).

How does forgiveness change our past and future? The explanation lies in the entangling power of memory. We not only are aware of our inner failings, shortcomings, and acts of rebellion, but we *remember* them. And when we remember them, we are gripped by a sense of guilt and powerlessness. All our inadequacies are stored in our memory; they shout at us, convincing us that we have failed, that we are failures, and that we will fail again if we dare try to follow God's will.

But the good news of forgiveness shouts back: God has taken away our sins. Christ's death on the cross dealt so powerfully with our failures that God says He won't even *remember* our sin (Heb. 10:17). And as testimony to the completeness of our release, the Bible adds "where these have been forgiven, there is no longer any sacrifice for sin" (Heb. 10:18).

You and I receive this amazing forgiveness when we trust Jesus as Savior, and all that Christ won for us on Calvary becomes ours. We experience the reality of this forgiveness as we daily confess our sins to God and open our hearts to God's Spirit, who will cleanse us from impurity and release us from the burden of our past. Then, with past sins put behind us and forgotten, we move on thankfully to live an increasingly holy life.

This is how we experience God's forgiveness. We accept God's Word that the release promised in Jesus is ours. We confess fresh sins as they are committed—and then we forget them, for they have been taken away.

Extending forgiveness to others. A life lived in touch with God is lived in a personal, ongoing experience of divine forgiveness. And a life lived in touch with God is lived in a personal, ongoing expression of that forgiveness in our relationships with others.

The New Testament makes a delicate but important

distinction here. God's forgiveness is *aphiēmi:* He "sends away" our sin. But human forgiveness is always *charizomai:* we "deal graciously" with sin. You and I cannot send away the sin of another; only Jesus can remove sin. But we can be gracious to each other. We can be "kind and compassionate to one another, forgiving each other, just as in Christ God forgave [us]" (Eph. 4:32).

The New Testament makes it clear that it is not optional for Christians to be forgiving; it is mandatory that we forgive others. We repeatedly are reminded that we must live with others in grace: we are to adopt a forgiving lifestyle.

The theme is developed in a series of stories in Matthew 18. Jesus was giving private instruction to His disciples, teaching them about spiritual greatness. He called a child to Him. The child responded immediately and came to Jesus (Matt. 18:2). This child, Jesus told the Twelve, is our model of greatness, for the child was humble and responded immediately to Christ's word. To live in union with God, we must, like that child, humble ourselves and respond unhesitatingly to the voice of the Lord (Matt. 18:3–5).

How can we develop and retain such childlike qualities? With a warning that underlines the importance of this teaching (Matt. 18:10–14), Jesus tells three stories about forgiveness.

Find and restore the wanderer. The story of the lost sheep (Matt. 18:10–14) reminds us that we, like sheep, tend to go astray. When even one sheep wanders from the flock, the shepherd searches for it, and when it is found, the shepherd is "happier about that one sheep than about the ninety-nine that did not wander off."

As we live with others, as Martha lives with her husband, we must *expect* that they will wander. And when a person does, we are to mimic the shepherd: we are to take the initiative, to seek the wanderer, and to restore the relationship. When the relationship is restored, the emotion that floods the heart is joy—not recrimination, not bitterness, not remembered hurt, but happiness.

Keenly aware of how the Lord has forgiven us, we are to forgive others. Grateful for how the Lord has restored us to full relationship with Him, we are to restore others by reaching out to them, offering a forgiveness that neither condemns or demands repayment.

Forgive repeatedly. A second story follows immediately (Matt. 18:15–22). The believing community is like a family of children. As in any family, Christians are sure to hurt each other and to sin against each other just as children are sure to bicker. Jesus teaches that when hurts and sins distort a family relationship, we are to go to the other person, point out the sin, and let forgiveness flow.

Peter, concerned about how often we are hurt by others, asked Jesus "How many times shall I forgive. . . ? Up to seven times?" (Matt. 18:21).

"Not seven times," Jesus answered, "but seventy-seven times" (Matt. 18:22). Forgiveness must be limitless. In the family of God we are to forgive as often as we are hurt: again and again and again and again. We are to forgive as freely as God, in Christ, has forgiven us.

Forgive compassionately. Jesus concludes with a story about a debtor who owed a ruler several million dollars. Unable to pay the overwhelming debt, the debtor begged for more time. The ruler, moved by compassion, forgave the entire debt!

Later the debtor went to a servant who owed him a few dollars. The debtor demanded repayment of the small debt, and when the servant was unable to pay, the debtor threw the servant in prison!

When the ruler learned about this, he called in the debtor whose debt he had canceled. "You wicked servant," the king shouted. "I canceled all that debt of yours because you begged me to. Shouldn't you have had mercy on your fellow servant as I had on you?" (Matt. 18:32–33).

The meaning is clear. God has forgiven the enormous debt we couldn't possibly pay. He did it out of compassion, asking us for nothing of what we rightfully owed. How can we, who experience such forgiveness from God, withhold our compassion from others, whose sins against us are so much less than our offenses against the Lord?

When we realize the depth of God's forgiveness of us, we only can respond by forgiving others. To live a human life in union with God means to respond to God's forgiveness by forgiving others.

Jesus and Forgiveness

Jesus understands the pain that we feel when others hurt us. He too was hurt. He came to earth to show people God's love, but very few people even bothered to listen to Him. The religious leaders rejected both Him and His message. Many people hurt Him with callous indifference to His powerful message of reconciliation and redemption.

Jesus too knows what it's like to live with others who are sinful. His disciples, the men in whom He invested much of His earthly ministry, often disappointed Him with their thickheadedness and their petty arguments about who would be the greatest in His kingdom. One of His own disciples denied even knowing Him, and another disciple betrayed Him to an angry mob.

Jesus knew every pain that can be caused by the sin in others. He knew, not just as God, but as a human being. He experienced every insensitivity, every rejection, every hostility, every antagonism, every pain that we experience. And through it all, Jesus continued to love. He continued to give. He continued to serve. Ultimately Jesus took His place alone on Calvary's cross. Even on the cross, at the height of His rejection by other people, He chose not to focus on His own pain but to extend forgiveness to His enemies: "Forgive them, for they do not know what they are doing" (Luke 23:34).

Jesus' teaching about forgiveness carries a special sense of authenticity. The Gospel's emphasis on forgiveness reflects our Lord's deep understanding of the human condition. He knows more fully than we ever could what it means to live with sinners. When others hurt us, we can look to Christ's example, realizing that we have been called to live His kind of life.

And we need to understand one of Jesus' often-misunderstood teachings about forgiveness. He told His followers, "If you forgive men when they sin against you, your heavenly Father will also forgive you. But if you do not forgive men their sins, your Father will not forgive your sins" (Matt. 6:14–15). We are troubled by this teaching. Is our forgiveness really conditional, based on how we treat others? What about the promises of full forgiveness to all who believe? What about forgiveness won by Christ's blood, contingent only on our willingness to receive God's grace?

We need to realize that Jesus is speaking not of salvation here but of psychological reality. Forgiveness is like a coin; it has two sides—receiving forgiveness and extending forgiveness. These two dynamics must be part of a unified whole. The same awareness—the awareness of our own sin—that leads us to ask God to forgive us leads us to forgive others. When we are aware of the the depth of our own sin, we know we are no better than anyone else. When we realize that we are all sinners, we accept that we all need forgiveness, from God and from each other. We stop demanding perfection, from ourselves and from others. In receiving God's forgiveness, we confess the reality of our sin and accept His grace. And in extending forgiveness to others, we affirm the reality of their sin and extend to them the grace we received from our Lord.

Both receiving and extending forgiveness demand humility. When we humbly receive God's forgiveness, we humbly can accept the sin in others. When we feel the joy and freedom of God's mercy to us, we can forgive others with the same compassion and mercy.

Practicing Forgiving Grace

How do we grow in our capacity to show compassion for others, and how do we extend forgiveness when they sin against us? Here are some keys.

Convert pain to compassion. When people hurt you, use the pain redemptively. Love "is not easily angered, it keeps no record of wrongs" (1 Cor. 13:5) Why? Because when we love, we look beyond our own hurts to the other person's need. Perhaps someone makes a cutting remark about you. Instead of getting angry, let that remark sensitize you to the person's own pain. Perhaps your son thoughtlessly disregards your needs. Instead of thinking "if he really loved me, he would . . . " or instead of feeling resentment, let that thoughtlessness sensitize you to his immaturity and need to grow.

You'll find this is easier if you consciously identify with the person who hurts you. "There, but for the grace of God go I" is more than a saying; it is a profound truth. Identifying with others does not excuse them, but it fosters humility in us. It enables us to sense the frailness of the humanity we share, helping us drain away the anger and replace it with compassion.

Determine when to confront—and when not to. When we deal with sin in other people, either we can put up with it or we can confront them about it. The Bible encourages us to use both responses.

"As God's chosen people, holy and dearly loved" we are to "clothe [ourselves] with compassion, kindness, humility, gentleness and patience" (Col. 3:12). We are to *"bear with each other* and forgive whatever grievances [we] may have against [each other]" (Col. 3:13a, italics added).

The words "bear with" come from the Greek *anecho-mai,* which means "tolerate" or "put up with." We are not called to correct every flaw in our brother or sister. Some flaws we simply must live with, tolerating them as the person grows and matures in faith. Even though we may have valid reasons to be upset about the sin, sometimes we must put up with the flaws, accepting the person in spite of the sin.

Bearing with someone's sin is not easy. Tolerating someone's faults doesn't mean we overlook these sins as if they didn't matter. Bearing with someone's sin means recognizing that the sin matters but choosing not to let it get in the way of our relationship. This kind of forgiveness requires great compassion and patience. But when we look at God's great patience in bearing with our sin, we can more easily bear with the sins of others. Bearing with someone's sin demands constant prayer. Only God can give us the endurance and grace we need to put up with annoying sin in other people.

The second option is to confront the person with his or her sin. Jesus said, "If your brother sins against you, go and show him his fault, just between the two of you" (Matt. 18:15a). Confronting someone with his or her sin helps the person recognize and deal with a serious sin in his or her life. If the other person will recognize the behavior as sin, he or she can confess that sin to God and experience cleansing.

When we confront a person with sin, we must confront lovingly, not self-righteously or condemningly. The purpose of confrontation always must be for the other person's good, not for our good. We never must confront a person just because we are tired of living with his or her flaws. Our motive must not be selfish. We must not confront a person just to get something off our own chest. Remembering the depth of our own sin will help us be compassionate when we confront someone else with his or her sin.

How can we tell whether to confront or whether to put up with another's faults? Most often we will need to rely on the Spirit's individual leading. But a general principle can help us remain sensitive to His voice: If the other person's actions are so disturbing to us that we find it impossible to love or if we can no longer see the good in the other person because of the faults, then we probably need to speak to him or her about the sin. If on the other hand we can maintain a positive and loving attitude—if the other person's actions have not alienated us or put unusual strain on our relationship—the best course is to put up with the flaw and forgive.

To some extent, our own spiritual maturity and sensitivity is measured by our growing capacity to bear with the flaws of others. As we do grow, we'll discover a special joy that comes when we "keep no record of wrongs" but love others freely, even when they stumble over the tangled roots of inward sin.

TO THINK ABOUT AND DO

1. Have you ever received forgiveness from a person whom you had hurt deeply? Recall and describe the experience. How did you feel? Was it easy or hard to receive their forgiveness?

   Have you ever extended forgiveness to a friend or loved one who hurt you deeply? Describe that experience. How did you feel? Which was easier, to extend forgiveness or to receive it? Why?

2. Write in your own words why a person who lives in touch with God will grow in his or her capacity to forgive. Compare your response to the responses of others.

3. Read over the introductory story about Martha and Ken. Martha may have avoided the situation either by putting up with his flaws or by confronting Ken about them. Which course do you think she should have taken? Which would you take in a similar situation?

   What do you think Ken could have done differently? What flaws in Martha did he have put up with? Do you see anything he might have needed to confront?

   Why do family relationships, which have the greatest potential for intimacy, also seem to have such potential for pain?

4. Examine your own relationships with others. Write down the names of people whose actions tend to hurt or upset you. Next to the names, write down the specific actions that bother you most. Then pray about these people and actions. Try to identify with the other person. Examine your reactions. What do they tell you about yourself? As you pray, listen for God's voice. Are you to put up with the other person's flaws and keep on loving despite them? Or are you to confront them lovingly as an aid to their spiritual growth?

8

HOLINESS

"Holiness kind of scares me."

"What do you mean, scares you?" one of our group asked.

"Well, that verse that says 'be holy, because I am holy,' seems too much for us. We've just talked about sin in our lives. How can we be holy if we all are sinners?"

"Would it help if we talked about personal morality instead of holiness?"

"It sure would be easier for me! I know we're supposed to live good moral lives. But holiness. Well, that always seems to be so much more."

"They might seem to be different. But I think we'll find that they're not as different as most of us might think."

The Old Testament and Personal Morality†

You may be surprised to know that the word *moral* appears only once (James 1:21) in the New International Version of the Bible, and the word *morality* isn't found in this version at all! Still, the Bible has much to say about morality.

Morality and evil. Morality is associated closely with the word *evil,* conveyed in the Hebrew word *ra'*. Moral evil is any act that violates God's intentions for human beings. The Bible speaks of actions that are "evil in the eyes of the Lord" (see Num. 32:13; Judg. 2:11; 1 Kings 15:26; etc.). Good and evil are rooted in God's very nature, and it is His evaluation of moral acts that defines each. While you and I never will be good in an absolute sense, as God is good, we still are called on to be good and holy persons, living up to God's expectations for us.

The Hebrew *ra'* speaks not only of actions that violate

†This discussion is based on chapter 16, pp. 196–197.

God's standard but also of the consequences of these actions. In this sense evil is the distress, the tragedy, the physical and emotional harm that flow from wrong moral choices. Moses had this meaning in mind when he spoke to Israel after he had reviewed the Law, "See, I set before you today life and prosperity [*tôb*, "good"], death and destruction [*ra'*, "evil"]" (Deut. 30:15).

Morality and holiness in the Old Testament. The Old Testament links holiness with two of God's traits: His power and His moral nature. God's power, or splendor, is often displayed in judgment, as is illustrated in His response to Aaron's sons who violated the ritual regulations governing Israel's worship. God told Moses:

> "Among those who approach me
> I will show myself holy;
> in the sight of all the people
> I will be honored" (Lev. 10:3).

Then God sent fire to consume the men who had treated Him with contempt by ignoring His commands about worship rituals. God's holiness is like fire: sometimes it shines in powerful brilliance; other times it devours what is not pure.

Leviticus 19 focuses on a moral dimension of holiness. God tells Moses, "Speak to the entire assembly of Israel and say to them: 'Be holy because I, the LORD your God, am holy'" (Lev. 19:2). The commands that follow are not ritual but moral in character. God tells the people that because He is the Lord their God, He does not want them to steal, lie, defraud each other, slander one another, take revenge on each other, and so on. He sums up His commands by instructing them to love their neighbors. Here, and in many other passages, God's holiness is associated explicitly with His own moral character. His holiness is displayed in His concern for doing what is right and in His commitment to the welfare of all His creatures.

A third aspect of Old Testament holiness is linked to separation. What was holy was separated or set apart to God's service. The priests, the altar, the temple and its furnishings were holy to the Lord; they were different from secular persons, places, and things. Israel itself was a holy nation, set apart for God's service. The Sabbath day was holy too, different from all other days, set aside for rest. God's anger had flared out against Aaron's sons because they failed to distinguish between the holy and the profane, the clean and the unclean.

Jesus and Holiness

Jesus, in His human life, reflected His Father's holiness. He exhibited both His Father's brilliant splendor and His moral purity. But Jesus also demonstrated a new dynamic in holiness. In His time on earth, Jesus confronted a perverted holiness that He saw in the Pharisees of His day.

The Pharisees' concept of holiness was linked closely to the Old Testament concept of separation, of ritual cleanness. Holiness to them meant separating the clean from the unclean, the holy from the profane. They not only tried to obey every meticulous detail of the Law, but they also wrote hundreds of other laws, defining what was acceptable and unacceptable behavior. The Pharisees were compulsive in their holiness. They were proud of their ability to keep every command.

The Pharisees clashed with Jesus because He seemed to be unconcerned about the strict separation they practiced. They watched Him closely, pouncing on Him whenever He strayed from their strict interpretation of the Law.

For instance, one day Jesus healed a person on the Sabbath, that holy day set aside for rest. The Pharisees were upset. "Is it lawful to heal on the Sabbath?" they asked, shocked. Jesus replied, "If any of you has a sheep and it falls into a pit on the Sabbath, will you not take hold of it and lift it out? How much more valuable is a man than a sheep! Therefore it is lawful to do good on the Sabbath" (Matt. 12:10b–12).

Another time Jesus went to a party at the home of Levi, a tax collector. Levi invited his friends: "many tax collectors and 'sinners.'" When the Pharisees saw this, they were shocked again. As holy men, they kept themselves isolated from such people, unwilling to be contaminated by association with them. After all, the Law called for separation of the holy and unholy, the clean and unclean. Later Jesus told the Pharisees, "It is not the healthy who need a doctor, but the sick. I have not come to call the righteous, but sinners" (Mark 2:15–17).

The clash between the Pharisees' idea of holiness and Jesus' idea is illustrated in an incident at the home of Simon, the Pharisee. As Jesus and the others reclined at the table, a "woman who had lived a sinful life" slipped in. Weeping, she began to wet Jesus' feet with her tears. She wiped His feet with with her hair and poured an expensive, perfumed ointment on them.

The Pharisee was scandalized. He thought, "If this man were a prophet, he would know who is touching him and what kind of woman she is—that she is a sinner" (Luke 7:39b). Simon assumed that a truly holy man would quickly withdraw from a sinner's touch.

Jesus confronted Simon and told him a parable of two men, each of whom had had debts canceled. Which would most appreciate the lender: one whose small debt had been forgiven or one whose overwhelming obligation had been canceled? The Pharisee answered correctly. Then Jesus said to the woman, "Your sins are forgiven. Your faith has saved you; go in peace" (Luke 7:48, 50).

To Jesus the touch of a sinner was not repugnant or wrong. But to the Pharisee, who saw holiness as separating the holy from the unholy, the clean from the unclean, such contact was repulsive. The Pharisees applied their concern for ritual cleanness to their relationships with people, and the result was a spiritual pride that judged others unworthy of love or compassion, or even unworthy of the most casual association.

Jesus lived among these Pharisees and introduced a *new morality*. While the Pharisees drew back from sinners; Jesus reached out to them. While the Pharisees' holiness was rooted in their adherence to rigid rules, Jesus' holiness was rooted in His union to God and His commitment to please God. While the Pharisees separated themselves from anything unclean, Jesus chose to live *in the midst* of a sin-stained world, *with* sinners.

The same God who expressed His holiness in consuming fire also expressed His holiness in many of His commandments instructing His people to love their neighbors! *Jesus based His view of holiness on the divine command to care.*

We must realize that while personal holiness demands separation from sin, it calls for active involvement with sinners and with the world. We must be careful not to fall into the trap of the Pharisees. We are not to think of holiness in terms of the "do nots" that set good people apart from sinners. The needs of people are still more important than keeping the Sabbath. The sinner is still to be sought out rather than to be pushed away.

While Jesus rejected sin, He never rejected the sinner. He rejected evil but became actively involved in the lives of sinners. Although Jesus was involved with sinners, He was never tainted by their sin. In Jesus' example we see the true nature of holiness and personal morality.

Living a Holy Life

Living a holy life in union with God means that we not only will resist what is evil, but we also will choose to do what is right. The Epistles help us see these two dynamics of personal holiness and morality. We live in a sinful world, and yet we choose not to sin: we refrain from those things God's Word identifies as wrong. At the same time, we actively choose to do good. We commit ourselves to be caring, compassionate people, eager to help, eager to heal. *Only an active commitment to do good captures the dynamic morality of Scripture. A truly holy life is a fully involved life.*

We see this twofold dynamic in so many passages. Colossians 3 calls on us to *reject* "sexual immorality, impurity, lust, evil desires and greed" (Col. 3:5b), but *put on* "compassion, kindness, humility, gentleness and patience" (Col. 3:12).

In Ephesians 4:17–30 Paul lists characteristics of an immoral life and concludes, "Get right of all bitterness, rage and anger, brawling and slander, along with every form of malice. Be kind and compassionate to one another, forgiving each other, just as in Christ God forgave you. Be imitators of God, therefore, as dearly loved children and live a life of love, just as Christ loved us and gave himself up for us as a fragrant offering and sacrifice to God" (Eph. 4:31–5:2). We must get rid of destructive behavior so that we can be free to live a life that reflects our Father.

Peter also teaches us about the balance between resisting evil and choosing good. In each example, it is as if Peter says in one breath, "Get rid of this, *but also* do this."

These two lists from the Epistles summarize what we are to put off so that we can put on actions and attitudes in harmony with God's will. Remember as you read these two lists that the same Lord who calls us to resist evil also *empowers* us to say no to evil. The same Lord who calls us to do good *enables* us to do what pleases God. He does not demand what is impossible. He shows us His will and then gives us the ability to do it.

Negatives of holiness/morality	Positives of holiness/morality
Do not conform to the evil desires you had when you lived in ignorance (1 Peter 1:14).	Just as he who called you is holy, so be holy in all you do (1 Peter 1:15).
Rid yourselves of all malice and all deceit, hypocrisy, envy, and slander of every kind (1 Peter 2:1).	Crave pure spiritual milk, so that by it you may grow up in your salvation (1 Peter 2:2).
Abstain from sinful desires, which war against your soul (1 Peter 2:11b).	Live such good lives among the pagans that, though they accuse you of doing wrong, they may see your good deeds and glorify God on the day he visits us (1 Peter 2:12).

We are to put off:

    sexual immorality
    impurity
    greed
    obscenity
    lust
    evil desires
    anger
    malice
    filthy language
    debauchery
    hatred
    fits of rage
    selfish ambition
    envy
    drunkenness
    orgies and the like
    slander
    lies

We are to put on:

    gentleness
    kindness
    compassion
    forgiveness
    self-sacrifice
    patience
    doing good
    love
    peacefulness
    kindness
    goodness
    speaking the truth
    gentleness
    bearing with others

These positive moral qualities will be expressed in our relationships with fellow Christians and non-Christians alike. For in our life with God, these sum up both the holiness to which we are called and the morality we are expected to live.

Growth in Personal Holiness

What can help us keep true holiness in focus as we seek to respond to God's call?

Self-examination. How do we think of holiness and morality? Do we stress the "don'ts" and separation? While turning from sin is important in maintaining moral purity, we can't afford to assume that Christian morality is negative in nature. That notion leads all too often to spiritual pride and self-satisfaction that judges and disdains sinners. Instead, we are to be like Jesus, who involved Himself actively with sinners so that He could show them the way to His Father. Our holy God is committed to doing what is good. Living a holy life in touch with God means sharing that commitment and expressing holiness and morality through loving involvement with others.

Meditate on Jesus. We need to read and reread the Gospels until we can visualize Jesus in His relationships with others. We need to see Him laughing comfortably with sinners, relaxed and friendly. We need to sense the warmth that won their affection. We need to imagine Jesus accepting the touch of Mary the prostitute, even in the Pharisee's home. Jesus was neither threatened by the presence of sinners nor attracted by their sin. Instead, He was free—free to reach out and love even persons whose sins must have repelled Him.

As we meditate on Jesus, we need to imagine Him in our situations. We need to picture Him walking in our shoes. As we learn who He is, we begin to understand what He would do and say. And we gradually find ourselves freed to follow His example. We gradually realize that Jesus *is* walking in our shoes. He is reaching out through us, loving, caring—doing and being truly good.

We need to see others with renewed eyes. We need to look closely at our attitude toward the people we contact daily. Does a co-worker with a filthy mouth offend us? Has the immoral lifestyle of an acquaintance so repelled us that we condemn rather than care? If so, how wonderful to realize that holiness does not demand this kind of reaction at all! Holiness calls us instead to reach out, to seek, to pray for, and to care about persons whose real need is for our Christ, not our rejection.

Holiness, as we discover it in the Bible, need not frighten us at all. God's call to be holy is not a call to an impossible life. It is simply a call to choose what is good and to live a life of love.

TO THINK ABOUT AND DO

1. Read 1 Corinthians 5:1–15. How would you describe the Corinthians' view of holiness? How would you describe Paul's view of holiness? How does this passage reflect Jesus' approach to holiness. How does it reject the view of the Pharisees?

2. From the list of positive qualities we are urged to put on, select two in which you want to grow. Jot down every way you envision these qualities can be expressed in your life. Try to picture how each might shape your relationship to different people. As you build an image of this quality, ask God to express Himself through that quality in you.

3. Read through one of the Gospels. Select two incidents that show Jesus either relating to sinners or acting in ways that scandalized the Pharisees. Meditate on these incidents. What is God showing you about holiness? What is the Lord calling you to do or be?

9

SUFFERING

"He said that Jesus took our suffering as well as our sin."
"Oh? And what did he mean by that?"
"Well, he said that God intends His children to be freed from all sickness and suffering. If a person claims the victory by faith, then the person no longer suffers. He said we can claim victory just as we claim salvation."
"What were the biblical grounds for his teaching?"
"Well, he said that healing is in the Atonement. That Isaiah 53, where it says 'by his stripes we are healed,' means just what it says. He said that just as we don't like to see our kids suffer, God doesn't want His children to suffer either."
"So if we suffer, it's our own fault?
"I guess so. At least, it's our fault if we don't have enough faith to claim healing."
"Now, that's what the radio preacher said. What do you think about it?"
"Well, I don't think he's right, but I'm not sure why. And what I wonder is, how can we stay in touch with God when we suffer? I know that when I hurt, I don't feel very close to Him."

That's a good question. How do we stay in touch with God when we suffer? We live in a tangled world in which we all experience grief and pain. If we want to live our lives in union with God, we need to understand how to respond to suffering when it comes.

Jesus and Suffering†

The Gospels show Jesus as a man who was actively involved with suffering people. When Jesus saw someone with a need, He acted immediately to relieve the pain. He healed, brought peace, and met needs. We wonder at His

†This discussion is based on chapter 14, pp. 178–180.

power and at His love. But perhaps we should pause to wonder at two other things.

First, we should wonder that suffering exists at all. We don't wonder. Suffering is so common to all human experience. We know that to be human means to be subject to weakness, to pain, to sickness. And we know that suffering is more than physical. Death tears loved ones from us. We experience rejection: our plans for marriage fall through, or we lose our jobs. We suddenly realize that our plans for the future are meaningless. We helplessly watch our children struggle financially. A thousand different experiences bring us in touch with pain and suffering. Suffering—both physical pain and our deep inner anguish—is so much a part of life that we seldom stop to wonder why God permits it at all.

Second, we should wonder that the person who was so quick to relieve the suffering of others was Himself subject to intense suffering. We need to focus our attention not on suffering *and* Jesus but on the suffering *of* Jesus.

It is not how Jesus acted to relieve the pain of others that helps us as we seek to live in union with God. It is how Jesus dealt with His own pain that helps us grasp the link between spirituality and suffering.

Most New Testament references to suffering are renderings of the Greek word *paschō,* which is used in relation to Jesus' death and events linked with it. We're forcefully reminded that Jesus suffered according to God's specific will (see Matt. 16:21; Mark 8:31; Luke 17:25; 24:26; Acts 17:3). Jesus' suffering was not accidental; it was divinely planned. It was purposive. Jesus suffered not because He was trapped in an impersonal, oppressive universe but because it was God's will for Him to suffer.

This fact alone tells us that we must develop a fresh perspective about suffering. Suffering isn't necessarily an experience from which God wants to deliver His children.

Suffering may be something that God specifically plans *for* them.

We, of course, know the good Jesus' suffering accomplished. Jesus suffered for us. He died in our place. By the anguish of His soul, Jesus has made us righteous and has won a place for us in heaven. Perhaps that's why we so often miss the point. If God decreed His Son's suffering and through it worked out His good plan, then unquestionably God *can* and sometimes *does* decree suffering for His children.

How did Jesus perceive His suffering, and how did He respond to it? What can we learn from His example?

The Gospels frequently use the word *paschō* in describing the events associated with Christ's death. For instance, in the anguish of Gethsemane, Jesus said to Peter, James, and John, "My soul is overwhelmed with sorrow to the point of death" (Matt. 26:38). Luke adds, "Being in anguish, [Jesus] prayed more earnestly, and his sweat was like drops of blood falling to the ground" (Luke 22:44).

Unimaginable torment and terror gripped Jesus at that moment. The pain of looking forward to the Cross, where the sinless Son of God would know the searing agony of being made sin for us (2 Cor. 5:21), seemed more than Christ could bear. Yet in His moment of anguish, Jesus reaffirmed His full commitment to God. "Not as I will, but as you will" (Matt. 26:39). In His time of suffering, Jesus surrendered Himself to the will of God.

The writer of Hebrews says, "He offered up prayers and petitions with loud cries and tears to the one who could save him from death, and he was heard because of his reverent submission" (Heb. 5:7). He was heard, but He found no relief from the suffering. Jesus was heard, but the agony of His death was itself part of God's answer. Jesus would rise again, but only after He fully had tasted suffering.

Peter describes Jesus' attitude: "When he suffered [at the

hands of evil men], he made no threats. Instead, he entrusted himself to him who judges justly" (1 Peter 2:23). Jesus surrendered Himself to God, confident that God is just and sure that God intended only good to come through His pain.

If we take Jesus as our model of the spiritual person, the one whose example we follow, we see in Him this perception: suffering is God's will. And we see this response: He prayed for release and submitted Himself to God.

Jesus expressed His desire for release in prayer. He surrendered His will to the will of God. Jesus entrusted Himself to God, sure that God is just, sure that His own suffering was intended for good.

The Pain-Filled Good

Jesus' response to suffering shows us that we are to view the believer's suffering not as something to be avoided at all costs but as a pain-filled good. The Old Testament hints at this in associating suffering and pain with the image of childbirth. Genesis 3 makes it clear that human pain and suffering are a direct result of sin (see Gen. 3:16–17). But both this passage and Romans 8:18–25 remind us that whatever its cause, pain is intended to give birth to good. As new life comes into this world only through the pangs of childbirth, so good often comes to us only through pain and suffering.

This view of suffering as a pain-filled good is developed most powerfully in 1 Peter. Here Peter calls on us to live a good life, knowing that "Whoever would love life and see good days must keep his tongue from evil and his lips from deceitful speech" (1 Peter 3:10).

Peter's argument is that God actively superintends the experiences of the good man, so that "who is going to harm you if you are eager to do good?" (1 Peter 3:13). But after stating this general principle, Peter goes on to look at the unusual case in which a person suffers for doing right (1 Peter 3:14). He first explains how to respond to unexpected and unmerited suffering: we are not to be afraid but to set Christ apart as Lord. That is, we are to acknowledge the sovereignty of God as that sovereignty is expressed in what we now experience. This enables us both to face suffering with hope and to witness to others who are surprised at our positive outlook despite our pain. Finally, we are to keep on doing good and to maintain a clear conscience (1 Peter 3:15–17).

Then Peter calls us to look at Jesus, the prime example of a person whose suffering was a clear injustice. Jesus did only good. Yet it was He, not those who sinned against Him, who suffered. But the suffering of Jesus was a pain-filled good. Through His suffering, Jesus brought us to God (1 Peter 3:18).

Peter's point is simply this. Viewed as a human event, Jesus' suffering was a tragic miscarriage of justice—an evil. But when seen from God's perspective, Jesus' suffering was both purposive and good. God *intended* Jesus to suffer so that through His suffering the whole world might be blessed.

And this is exactly how we are to view our suffering. Surely some of our suffering is merely a consequence of our sins. But sometimes we suffer unexpectedly, unjustly, through no fault of our own. When this happens, we are not to see our suffering as an evil, but as something that is purposive and good. We are to realize that God *intends* us to suffer, and we are to believe that through our suffering He intends to bring us—and others—good.

Christian Suffering

We should not look for ways to suffer. Yet when suffering comes, we should not view it as an enemy. As Christians, we can view suffering as God's gift. Through our sufferings He makes us strong. Christ calls us not only to follow in His steps but also to share in His sufferings and glory.

> It is commendable if a man bears up under the pain of unjust suffering because he is conscious of God. . . . If you suffer for doing good and you endure it, this is commendable before God. To this you were called, because Christ suffered for you, leaving you an example, that you should follow in his steps (1 Peter 2:19–21).

> Since Christ suffered in his body, arm yourselves also with the same attitude, because He who has suffered in his body is done with sin. As a result, He does not live the rest of his earthly life for evil human desires, but rather for the will of God (1 Peter 4:1–2).

> The God of all grace, who called you to his eternal glory in Christ, after you have suffered a little while, will himself restore you and make you strong, firm and steadfast (1 Peter 5:10).

> Now if we are children, then we are heirs—heirs of God and co-heirs with Christ, if indeed we share in his sufferings in order that we may also share in his glory. I consider that our present sufferings are not worth comparing with the glory that will be revealed in us (Rom. 8:17–18).

The New Testament also urges us to be joyful when we face suffering. Because we can be confident that God is behind our sufferings, using them to bring about good, we can be happy not only *in our sufferings* but also *because of our sufferings*.

> We also rejoice in our sufferings, because we know that suffering produces perseverance; perseverance, character; and character, hope (Rom. 5:3–4).

> Dear friends, do not be surprised at the painful trial you are suffering, as though something strange were happening to you. But rejoice that you participate in the

sufferings of Christ, so that you may be overjoyed when his glory is revealed (1 Peter 4:12–13).

To live a human life in union with God is to live with suffering—not as an evil, but as a pain-filled good. As God used the suffering of Jesus to accomplish His purposes, so our suffering, too, is linked with God's purposes.

So let's go back to the teaching of the radio preacher. He taught that the person who is really in touch with God will be delivered from sickness, suffering, and pain if that person claims the victory by faith. Although this teaching is attractive, it simply is not true. The spiritual person may suffer deeply. Christ suffered, and His suffering is an example, reminding us "that [we] should follow in his steps" (1 Peter 2:21b).

Actually, even the notion that parents always will try to release their children from suffering isn't true. What mom hasn't heard wails when a child is denied a candy bar? Who hasn't said no when a child wants to watch one more TV show at bedtime? We hear our child's cries. The pain is real to him or her. But we adults know that children cannot judge and do not understand. The pain we cause is for their good. It's a part of growing up. It's necessary if they are to mature. Why then should we expect God, our good Father, to indulge our every whim and permit us to avoid suffering that may be essential to our spiritual growth?

God's will for us always involves some suffering, for God wants us to grow in Christlikeness. As Paul writes in Philippians, "I want to know Christ and the power of his resurrection and the fellowship of sharing in his sufferings, becoming like him in his death, and so, somehow, to attain to the resurrection from the dead" (Phil. 3:10–11). In our suffering we participate in Christ's sufferings.

Through our suffering we can experience His resurrection power that lifts us beyond ourselves.

How then are we to deal with our suffering?

Expect suffering. None of us is immune. The Bible says don't "be surprised at the painful trial you are suffering, as though something strange were happening to you. But rejoice that you participate in the sufferings of Christ, so that you may be overjoyed when his glory is revealed" (1 Peter 4:12–13). When suffering comes, we need not resent it as some evil intruder. Instead, we are to welcome—yes, even welcome—suffering. When suffering comes, we need not ask "why me?" Instead, we can ask God, "What is your good will in this?"

Submit to God. When suffering comes, we are to submit to it as the will of God. This doesn't mean we can't pray for release. Jesus did. Paul tells of a time when he was afflicted by what he calls a "thorn in my flesh" (2 Cor. 12:7b). But we also must express our desire for God's will to be done. We must remain sure, as Jesus was, that God's will is perfect and acceptable and desirable. When we do submit, we will come to the place that Paul describes in 2 Corinthians. He says, "Three times I pleaded with the Lord to take it away from me. But he said to me, 'My grace is sufficient for you, for my power is made perfect in weakness.' Therefore I will boast all the more gladly about my weaknesses, so that Christ's power may rest on me. That is why, for Christ's sake, I delight in weaknesses, in insults, in hardships, in persecutions, in difficulties. For when I am weak, then I am strong" (2 Cor. 12:8–10).

When I am weak, I surrender to God's will. And when I surrender, He strengthens me.

Remember Jesus. What helps us come to this place of surrender is the conviction that Jesus is Lord. He who loves us is sovereign. He who suffered for us is the one who permits our pain. Because we know how much He loves us, we can accept our suffering from His hand. Because we know His love, we can believe that however pain-filled an experience may be, it is intended for our good.

TO THINK ABOUT AND DO

1. Think back over the last time you experienced significant suffering. Which of the Bible verses quoted in this chapter would have been of greatest help then? Which would you have dismissed or disliked?

2. The Book of Job tells the story of a man who suffered for no fault of his own. He could not reconcile his experience with what he thought of God. His tortured doubts and fears are expressed in the bulk of his Old Testament book.

   While Job's suffering came to an end, God offered no explanation of why He had permitted his pain. Ultimately Job grasped the fact that we can't understand God; we can only trust Him. With this realization came the restoration of Job's many blessings.

   How did Job's final response to God (Job 42) compare with Jesus' submission to His Father?

3. How are you suffering now? Based on the Scripture verses in this chapter, how can you respond to your suffering and to God?

   Write a prayer, expressing your thoughts, fears, and desires to God. Include in your prayer an expression of trust and submission. Offer this prayer to God whenever you feel the pressure of your situation. Ask God to help you rejoice in your suffering.

SERVANTHOOD

"When I think of a servant, I think of someone who is weak."

"For me, servanthood suggests surrender. I imagine some drab woman who slaves all the time around the house, doing whatever her husband or children demand. After all, a servant has no free will. Right?"

"I know what you mean. Being a servant isn't much of a position. It doesn't have much status, if you know what I mean."

"It sure doesn't pay very much."

"But why then does Jesus talk about servanthood in such a positive way?"

"There must be something really important about servanthood. But surrendering your own interests all the time seems a pretty tough way to live."

Servanthood in the Scriptures†

When we turn to the Bible, we see an entirely different perspective of servanthood. It's not that servanthood is easy or that the servant is appreciated. But the image of weakness, of giving up your will and surrendering personal desires to another person, isn't really accurate.

Servant/slave in the Old Testament. The Old Testament uses several Hebrew words to denote the servant or slave. One Hebrew word, '*ebed*, means either "servant" or "slave." The root means simply "to work" or "to serve." Depending on context, this service can be menial or important, performed willingly or under force.

Another verb, *šārat*, also means "to serve." But this word has a specific connotation. The service that *šārat*,

†This discussion is based on chapter 19, pp. 233–236.

indicates is important. The person served is one of high rank—a very important person or God Himself. A close personal relationship exists between the person serving and the person being served. And the service itself is significant: it involves matters of real concern.

Servant/slave in the New Testament. Two different word groups develop our understanding of servanthood in the New Testament. *Douleuō* means "to serve as a slave." This word implies subjection of the slave's will to the master's will. While *doulos* may be translated either "slave" or "servant," we need to note an important distinction. Although the New Testament speaks of believers as slaves (*doulos*), it clearly teaches that believers are not slaves of one another but slaves of Christ. We are to subject our wills to Jesus and to Him alone!

The other Greek term, *diakoneō,* means "to serve" by acting to meet the needs of others. The New Testament shows us many ways to serve each other, offering both material and spiritual help to others. *The Expository Dictionary of Bible Words* helps us grasp what it means to commit ourselves to serve others.[1]

Words in the *diakoneo* group denote the giving of personal help to others. A wide range of kinds of help are included, from serving at tables (Luke 10:40) to collecting funds for needy brethren (Acts 11:29; 2 Cor. 8:4) to sharing Christ's word (2 Tim. 4:11; 2 Cor. 8:4). It is a concept that includes all the ministries within the body of Christ—the exercise of spiritual gifts and all offices (1 Cor. 12:4–6). The noun "deacon" is applied to men and women holding office in the church (Rom. 16:1; Phil. 1:1; 1 Titus 3:8–13). Of particular importance is the example set by Jesus. *Diakoneo* and cognate words were used by Jesus when He spoke of serving, as when He said, "The Son of Man did

---

[1] Lawrence O. Richards, *The Expository Dictionary of Bible Words,* (Grand Rapids: Zondervan Publishing House, 1986), p. 552.

not come to be served, but to serve, and to give his life as a ransom for many" (Matt. 20:28).

In Greek thought, both slavery (submission of the will) and servanthood (helping others in need) were contemptible. The Greeks were concerned with themselves and their search for personal excellence. To look to the needs of others and to spend oneself for the sake of others was degrading.

But in Jesus we see both slavery and servanthood lifted up. Jesus surrendered His will to God the Father, and He spent Himself here on this earth to meet the needs of other people. Through Jesus we begin to realize that slavery and servanthood are not contemptible, no matter what people may believe. Instead, slavery and servanthood mark out a pathway to spiritual fulfillment.

This brief review of slavery and servanthood helps clarify several misconceptions held by people in our group:

First, *servanthood does not mean we surrender our will to our fellow Christians.* To serve others, we do not have to do whatever they want us to do. Instead, we are slaves of Christ. When we practice servanthood, we subject our will to God's will, which may lead us into conflict with family members, co-workers, or friends we try to help. When we face that conflict, we must remember that Jesus is Lord. We affirm His lordship by subjecting our will to Him—not to others.

Second, *servanthood does not imply low status.* Jesus, God Himself, chose servanthood as a way of life. Like the *šārat,* of the Old Testament, the Christian who chooses a life of servanthood ministers to persons who are truly important, for each human being is important to God. When we take the path of servanthood, we reach out to people around us, offering help that contributes to their wholeness.

Third, *servanthood does not imply compulsion.* The Christian who adopts the servants lifestyle does not *have* to do so. Our decision to live as servants comes as a free, personal response to Jesus and is motivated by loving concern for others.

Jesus, the Servant

To live a human life in union with God, we must follow in the steps of Jesus. From Jesus' example we learn what it means to be a biblical servant.

Already in the Old Testament, the writers portrayed Christ as the "servant of the Lord." In four separate passages Isaiah portrays Jesus, the servant.

Isaiah 41:1–9 introduces us to the servant who, filled with God's Spirit, walks humbly among the bruised and worthless of the earth. This servant will establish justice on earth and will become the key that releases life's captives.

Isaiah 49:1–6 continues the teaching. The servant recognizes that God has shaped Him and has called Him to a mission that will unveil God's splendor. Though the servant appears to fail, He will call Israel back to the Lord and bring salvation to humankind.

Isaiah 50:4–10 shows God speaking to His servant and guiding Him. The servant is totally obedient, even though obedience involves suffering: "I offered my back to those who beat me, my cheeks to those who pulled out my beard; I did not hide my face from mocking and spitting" (v. 6). But God was at work in the servant's suffering and would vindicate Him.

Finally, Isaiah 52:13–53:12 graphically portrays Jesus' death. God's servant is pierced for the transgressions of others, and through His suffering He brings others peace. It was God's eternal intention to make His servant's life a guilt offering for sins. Yet afterward, the servant is restored to life and sees the results of His suffering. The servant is exalted in His obedience.

As we study these passages, we learn not only about Jesus but also about servanthood. In Isaiah we see that the servant is motivated by a desire to please God. We note that the servant adopts a humble stance before others. We see that the servant is committed to do others good, often at the expense of personal suffering. And we see that the servant trusts and obeys the Lord.

A desire to please God, humility, a commitment to help others, a willingness to suffer, a reliance on God, unquestioning obedience to the Lord—this is what servanthood is all about. This is how Jesus lived His life. And this is the way of life He invites you and me to adopt.

In the New Testament, Jesus teaches His disciples about the importance of becoming servants. He told them that if they wanted to become great, they had to adopt the role of a servant. The true leader is not the person who gains power and attention but the person who abandons power for servanthood and authority for ministry.

> "You know that the rulers of the Gentiles lord it over them, and their high officials exercise authority over them. Not so with you. Instead, whoever wants to become great among you must be your servant, and whoever wants to be first must be your slave—just as the Son of Man did not come to be served, but to serve, and to give his life as a ransom for many" (Matt. 20:25b–27).

We read these words, and we study Isaiah's servant passages, but we still may have difficulty understanding servanthood. Perhaps that's why Matthew records an incident that seems to sum up servanthood in a single, focused event. The gospel record seems to indicate that this event happened immediately after Jesus had talked with His disciples about servanthood.

When Jesus had finished talking with His disciples, He

left Jericho and started His trip to Jerusalem, where crowds were waiting to cheer Him. And there His enemies crouched, waiting, plotting to kill Him. Already then Jesus knew the suffering that was coming. He knew that His followers would desert Him and flee. Already then, as He traveled to Jerusalem, He began to sense the agony that would crush Him in Gethsemane.

How hard it must have been for Jesus to walk the road that led directly to Calvary. As Jesus set out on this road, two blind men cried out to Him. The crowd didn't care about the blind men. The crowd told them to be still. Why bother this important Rabbi, this man about whom the whole country talked? Who did these two blind beggars think they were to demand the attention of the teacher? But the blind men cried out even louder.

And Jesus heard. He stopped and went back. In spite of His own burden, in spite of His inner pain, Jesus listened to their request. The Bible says, "Jesus had compassion on them and touched their eyes. Immediately they received their sight and followed him" (Matt. 20:34).

If you want to understand servanthood, fix your mind on the image of Jesus, stopping there on the dusty road from Jericho to Jerusalem. Picture Him—setting aside His own pain, ignoring His own needs, and responding to the needs of others. This is what servanthood involves, not forced service, but a caring that makes us willing to sacrifice for others as an act of obedience to our Lord and as act of love even for those who count for nothing in our world.

"I see. But it really bothers me."

"What bothers you?"

"Well, if you go out of your way to help others, I think they'll take advantage of you. This servanthood puts us in a vulnerable position."

"It seems that way to me too. What if you do serve someone and that person takes advantage of you? Suppose you work hard

on your job, and the boss promotes someone else who doesn't deserve it. Are you supposed to keep on working just as hard, even though your boss is unfair? It seems to me that a person who really tries to be a servant is almost sure to be taken advantage of!"

In Union with God

It's true that servanthood doesn't provide us much leverage in our relationship with others. But we need to remember a few things. For one thing, our goal is to live our human life in union with God, not to make sure we each get ours! Jesus, who lived the servant's life, paid a price of personal suffering. He was rejected, but He didn't strike back. He was hurt, but He didn't try to hurt others. And while His servanthood led to Calvary, it also led to resurrection and to glory.

When people take advantage of us, we must remember that we didn't choose servanthood as a way to meet our own ego needs; we chose it as a way to please God. We must be servants even when it is inconvenient and even when other people mistreat us. Peter discusses this attitude as he addresses the slaves of his day: "Slaves, submit yourselves to your masters with all respect, not only to those who are good and considerate, but also to those who are harsh" (1 Peter 2:18). And Paul gives similar instructions: "Slaves, obey your earthly masters with respect and fear, and with sincerity of heart, just as you would obey Christ. Obey them not only to win their favor when their eye is on you, but like slaves of Christ, doing the will of God from your heart. Serve wholeheartedly, as if you were serving the Lord, not men, because you know that the Lord will reward everyone for whatever good he does, whether he is slave or free. And masters, treat your slaves in the same way. Do not threaten them, since you know that he who is both their

Master and yours is in heaven, and there is no favoritism with him" (Eph. 6:5–9).

Paul and Peter instruct slaves to see their primary responsibility to Christ, not to their masters. Slaves served their masters *as a response to Jesus.* Thus, whether the master is considerate or harsh, the slave continues to offer wholehearted service. In the same way, the master too is responsible to Christ. The master is responsible to the Lord *to be considerate.* Each party in this human relationship has a contract, not with the other but with the Lord.

It is the same in our servanthood. Jesus has called us to live as servants who care about others and who seek to help them. Our contract is with Jesus. The people whom we serve may not appreciate us, and they may even take advantage of us. If we see servanthood as a contract with *them,* we're likely to feel violated and angry; we may even convince ourselves that their behavior releases us from any obligation to serve them.

But we have no contract with others. We are slaves only of Jesus. We submit only to Him. And when we serve others, it is to please God, to obey Him, and to follow in the footsteps of Jesus.

Certainly others will take advantage of us! Look what they did to Jesus. But whether or not others take advantage of us simply doesn't matter. Our contract is with Jesus, not with other people

Growth in Servanthood

How do we grow in the grace of servanthood as we live our human life in union with God?

Acknowledge servanthood as a divine calling. Jesus said, "Whoever wants to become great among you must be your servant, and whoever wants to be first must be your slave—just as the Son of Man did not come to be served, but to serve, and to give his life as a ransom for many"

(Matt. 20:26–28). We can begin by making a personal commitment to Jesus—a contract, if you will—that with His help, we will follow His example and spend our own lives in service to others.

Adopt a servant's attitude. Servanthood is not designed to meet ego needs. Paul describes the servant attitude: "Do nothing out of selfish ambition or vain conceit, but in humility consider others better than yourselves. Each of you should look not only to your own interests, but also to the interests of others" (Phil. 2:3–4). Paul notes that this attitude is Christ's attitude (Phil. 2:5).

In another series of instructions Paul adds, "Be devoted to one another in brotherly love. Honor one another above yourselves. . . . Share with God's people who are in need. Practice hospitality. . . . Do not be proud, but be willing to associate with people of low position. Do not be conceited" (Rom. 12:10, 13, 16b).

The picture here is one of great sensitivity to others. It is a picture of shifting the focus of our concern from ourselves to others. As we realize how important each human being is to God, we will gain great satisfaction in each contribution we can make to their life and growth.

So we need to establish priorities. What will we value in this life? What will we put first? Our desires and pleasures? Our plans? Even our needs? Or will we follow Jesus and be willing to put aside our own concerns out of compassion for others?

Accept suffering. Servanthood is not designed to meet our ego needs. While God values servants highly, they are not esteemed by the world or by some Christians. Servants are often the people who clean up after the meeting, not the people who stand on the stage to receive the adulation of the crowd. Servants often are not appreciated; sometimes they are taken advantage of and hurt by the very people they serve.

If we want to be servants, we must be willing to get

hurt. We must be willing to suffer to serve. We must be willing to carry our cross daily, as Jesus was willing to carry His.

And most important, we must visualize Jesus pausing on a dusty Palestinian road. We must sense the agony He felt as He looked ahead and saw the pain He would suffer for us. We must see Him setting aside that anguish as He was moved by compassion to ask two blind beggars, "What do you want me to do for you?"

We must follow in His footsteps.

TO THINK ABOUT AND DO

1. How can you express servanthood in your relationships? Make a list of specific actions and specific relationships. Select two or three people to serve this week. Share your list and your decisions with a friend who will encourage you and hold you accountable.

2. We can't serve others if we don't know their needs. One way we can learn how to serve others is to listen sensitively.

First, as you listen to someone, consciously ask yourself, "How does the person feel about that?" When you think you have identified feelings, comment: "That seems to make you feel sad (or worried or upset, etc.)." If you have correctly identified the feeling, the person is likely to say, "Yes, I really do feel sad," and the person may go on to share more. If you have been incorrect, the person is likely to say, "No, not sad. I guess I feel more disappointed than sad." And again the person probably will go on to share more, simply because you have expressed concern about how he or she feels.

This kind of listening and responding often leads to

expression of needs and concerns that otherwise would have remained hidden. And when we know needs and concerns, we can reach out with compassion and offer help.

3. As servants, our "contract" is with Jesus, not with other people.

   First, diagram this concept, showing your relationships to others and your relationship to the Lord. To whom are you a slave (*douleuō,* submission of the will) and to whom are you a servant (*diakoneō,* offering help as a service)?

   Second, discuss what happens when someone takes advantage of our servanthood. How does this affect our service?

4. Talk over with someone how you feel about servanthood. Is it attractive to you? What fears does it arouse? What reservations do you have? What do you think is the most powerful reason why a Christian might choose a life of servanthood? Ask the person to pray with you about your fears/reservations. Ask God to mold you into the kind of servant He wants you to be.